The Desert Remembers My Name

Camino del Sol
A Latina and Latino Literary Series

∴ ∴, ∴

The Desert Remembers My Name

On Family and Writing

Kathleen J. Alcalá

The University of Arizona Press
Tucson

The University of Arizona Press

Library of Congress Cataloging-in-Publication Data
Alcalá, Kathleen, 1954–
The desert remembers my name : on family and writing /
Kathleen J. Alcalá.
p. cm. — (Camino del sol)
Includes bibliographical references.
ISBN-13: 978-0-8165-2626-0 (hardcover : alk. paper)
ISBN-10: 0-8165-2626-5 (hardcover : alk. paper)
ISBN-13: 978-0-8165-2627-7 (pbk. : alk. paper)
ISBN-10: 0-8165-2627-3 (pbk. : alk. paper)
1. Alcalá, Kathleen, 1954– 2. Authors, American — 20th
century — Biography. 3. Mexican American women authors —
Biography. I. Title.
PS3551.L287Z46 2007
813'.54 — dc22
[B]   2006036430

Publication of this book is made possible in part by
the proceeds of a permanent endowment created with
the assistance of a Challenge Grant from the National
Endowment for the Humanities, a federal agency.

Manufactured in the United States of America on acid-free,
archival-quality paper.

12 11 10 09 08 07   6 5 4 3 2 1

My agony is exquisite
Come, show me how in bread and wine
This God gives of Himself to me.
—Sor Juana Inéz de la Cruz

∴

Contents

Acknowledgments

The epigram is from "Loa for the Auto sacramental" in *Sor Juana Inéz de la Cruz: Poems, Protest and a Dream*, Penguin Classics, 1997, translated by Margaret Sayers Peden.

I would like to acknowledge the following for previous publication of some of these essays:

Periodicals: *The Colorado Review, Creative Nonfiction, Exhibition, Halapid, The Raven Chronicles, Re-Markings, Salt River Review* (on-line), *The Seattle Times*. Anthologies: *One Wound for Another/Una herida por otra: Testimonios de Latinos in the U.S. through Cyperspace (11 septiembre de 2001–11 marzo de 2002)*, Claire Joysmith and Clara Lomas, editoras, Universidad Nacional Autónoma de México, 2005; *Fantasmas: Supernatural Stories by Mexican American Writers*, Rob Johnson, editor, Bilingual Press/Editorial Bilingüe, Arizona State University, Tempe, 2001; *Keeping a Journal You Love*, Sheila Bender, editor, Writer's Digest Books, 2001; *A Writer's Journal*, Sheila Bender, editor, Dell Publishing, 1997.

Plays: An adaptation of the novel *Spirits of the Ordinary* was produced by the Miracle Theatre of Portland, Oregon, May 2003. Written by Kathleen Alcalá and Olga Sánchez, the excerpt is published with permission from Olga Sánchez.

"When Do You Sing?" was produced for radio by Jack Straw Productions, and aired on KUOW Public Radio on December 5, 2001.

The interview "The Transforming Eye of Kathleen Alcalá," by Rob Johnson, Web site of the American Center for Artists, www.americanartists.org, 1999, published with permission from Rob Johnson.

Thanks to the patient and helpful readers, Lisa D. Chavez and Emmy Pérez, and the editors at the University of Arizona Press.

❖ I ❖
My Week as a Mexican

My Week as a Mexican

My parents always told me I was Mexican. I was Mexican because they were Mexican. This was sometimes modified to "Mexican American," since I was born in California, and thus automatically a U.S. citizen. But, my parents said, this, too, was once part of Mexico. My father would say this with a sweeping gesture, taking in the smog, the beautiful mountains, the cars and houses and fast-food franchises. When he made that gesture, all was cleared away in my mind's eye to leave the hazy impression of a better place. We were here when the white people came, the Spaniards, then the Americans. And we will be here when they go away, he would say, and it will be part of Mexico again.

Although he was originally from the town of San Julian in Jalisco, Mexico, my father put down deep roots in East Highlands, California, around 1918. This was an unincorporated community of orange pickers and railroad workers outside of Redlands, in Southern California. Having lived there since the age of seven, he felt completely at home, and despite the deep poverty in which he was raised and his experiences with the racism of that time and place, my father seemed to think that it was all temporary, that all would be made right in the end. This optimism has allowed him to live into his nineties.

Each summer we piled into our station wagon — my parents, my two older sisters, and I — and drove two-and-a-half days to Chihuahua, Mexico, to stay with my mother's sister and her family. We all looked forward to it, I think, as an escape from our carefully measured lives in San Bernardino. In Chihuahua, anything could happen, and it was usually beautiful, delicious, delightful. Much to my father's satisfaction, it was also usually paid for by my uncle. It was like living your life in black and white most of the year, then spending two weeks living it in full color. There were band concerts in the park, fireworks available all year round, and delicious meals both at my aunt and uncle's house and in restaurants. It meant mango *paletas* and a piñata for my birthday, which was celebrated jointly with one of my cousins, and trips to the Santa Helena river.

As we got older, I could see that my five cousins were very different from us. While they loved American popular music — my cousin did a pretty good Elvis imitation — and comic books, I could tell that they lived by rules and regulations, social nuances, that did not coincide with ours. By the time we were teenagers, it was clear that our lives were on very different trajectories, directions determined, in large part, by which side of the border we lived on. I struggled to understand the political discussions between my father and my uncle, and my cousin Danny's profound anger and frustration with the government after the massacre of student demonstrators in 1968. There was unrest in the United States as well, but I could not believe that the Mexican government could do such things to its own people in a modern age. Danny died shortly after that of scarlet fever that was incorrectly diagnosed, a tragedy so great for the family that even today I cannot describe it.

I had a "twin" cousin named Ruth, born a week before me. Once a year, all through our growing up, our heights, our coloring, our coordination, charm, and precociousness were compared. Ruth always took the honors — taller, lighter skinned, more graceful, possessed of an innate dignity and charm that earned her the nickname La Princesa from her four siblings.

One of my earliest memories is visiting Mexico City with my cousins. Each family had a blue-and-white Ford station wagon. We went to the zoo and saw giraffes. We were about two years old, approaching three, for we have late-August birthdays. I remember that Ruth was already toilet trained, and so able to wear frilly panties. Whether she was drawing attention to this or not, I don't know. I only remember that I was acutely conscious of my inferiority in this matter.

That was also the trip on which we were in a major earthquake in Mexico City. I was sleeping on the floor of a hotel room when the sound of the closet door swinging open and shut, open and shut, woke me. My mother and her sister were sitting on the edge of the bed, their arms around each other. My father was not around. I asked what was going on.

"Oh, it's just an earthquake," said my aunt. "Go back to sleep."

So I did. Since we lived on the San Andreas fault in California, I was used to earthquakes. Only later would I learn the extent of the damage, and that my father was considered a hero because he had kept people from running out into the street, where others were killed by the stonework that fell from the exteriors of buildings.

By the time we were twelve, I had caught up to my cousin Ruth in height, but she had begun to develop the womanly curves that would attract the eye of her future husband, Felipe. Ruth's best friend, Gloria, was married on her fifteenth birthday. Ruth married on her eighteenth, and I was one of six bridesmaids in the all-white wedding — white dresses, white bunting, the entire inside of the church blanketed in white gardenias. The sickly-sweet smell was overpowering. I think Felipe's aunt designed the wedding, and the lack of color emphasized Felipe's dark good looks and maturity — several years older than we were. I kept the bridesmaid dress for a few years, but the only occasion for which it would have been suited was a coronation. With the end of the sixties, the formal dress had become passé.

The idea of marriage, much less married sex, was too much for me to even contemplate, and I remember thinking how glad I was it wasn't me.

It was a fairy-tale wedding for La Princesa, followed by a honeymoon on which she became pregnant. Her mother, my aunt, had told her that Norforms, a vaginal suppository, were a form of birth control. At eighteen, Ruth delivered a little girl in Piedras Negras, Mexico, close to the Texas border, where her husband worked for an American mining company. It was a difficult birth, with the assistance of a midwife. Due to oxygen deprivation, Carla was born with cerebral palsy and will require twenty-four-hour care for the rest of her life. Until recently, Ruth and her family lived in "The American Compound" — housing owned by the mining company outside of Chihuahua. Over thirty years later, Ruth continues to care for a strong and vibrant Carla, her other children grown and gone.

This has been my experience with Mexico — both a fairy tale and a stern taskmaster that, while gracious, has no patience for the romanticism or idealism it is so easy to bring to such a beautiful country.

My visit to Mexico City, forty years later, while researching my novel, *Treasures in Heaven*, brought back both of these views. It was the first time I had traveled to Mexico by myself as an adult. Naturally, my father forbade me to go, since I would probably be kidnapped by drug dealers. I have since joked that none of my research trips are official until my father forbids me to go.

A few years earlier, when my son was five months old, I had traveled to Chihuahua with him and my Anglo-American husband. This had resulted in the interesting charade of people outside of the family addressing my husband in Spanish, my translating, and then answering in Spanish, and the next line being addressed again to my husband, in Spanish. It was like the *Saturday Night Live* skit of closed-captioning for the hearing impaired, where someone in a little circle in the corner yelled out the news.

Since I was by myself this time, people had to address me directly. They were unfailingly polite and kind, even when they really wanted me to go away. As a woman in my forties, I was the age of most of their mothers, so they could not help but be polite to me. In my persistence, I was American. Told that a certain book or document was missing, inaccessible, or at a different location, I simply went on to the next thing on my list. Eventually, the librarians and archivists and receptionists would surrender and give me something to work with.

They also, in some cases, gave me their own stories, and asked me for mine as well. After all the trouble of getting through security into the Jewish archives, the receptionist told me that no one was in that day who could help me. After I inquired about some photos on her desk, and she proudly described her family's historic relationship to the Jewish community in Mexico City, the receptionist showed me some unpublished academic papers that provided invaluable information. In this way, I was Mexican, for this was the way I had been brought up—to do business with someone, you had to know who they were, who their people were. I was prepared for this with pictures of my family, stories about my extended family and ancestors, and copies of my own books in Spanish.

One day, after a visit to the Colégio de México, a policeman secured a little green taxi ("Don't take the little green taxis!") for me after the car from the hotel where I was staying refused to come back for me. I insisted that he write down the license of the taxi in case I was never seen again. As I climbed into the back seat, the driver said,

"Are you a Christian?" I looked up to see that, where the front right seat of the Volkswagen had been removed, as is the custom, he had set up a tiny shrine to the Virgin of Guadalupe. It was a sequined image in full color, with a cloth rose laid at her feet. I proceeded to tell him the story of my mother's family, Jews become Catholics become Protestants, as a way of gently telling him that I was not Catholic. He seemed calm about that, something I'm not sure would have been true even twenty years earlier. I was expecting him to proselytize, maybe hand me a brochure and ask for a donation. Now I think he may have asked because I did not cross myself upon entering the car, something most of his fares probably do if only out of sheer terror of the Mexico City traffic.

As in my early visits to Chihuahua, I felt set apart by my duality, yet invisible. During my travels as an adult — both in Mexico and in Europe — people always assume I am a native. Maybe it has something to do with my one travel rule — no white shoes. I felt, in some way, protected during this visit, perhaps in the same way that we were spared years earlier during the earthquake. Although I received a distinct, unspoken message that my visit to the pyramid at Tepotzlán needed to be brief, I never felt unsafe or unwanted. Powers were in effect that said, "Observe, but don't touch." And so, I did.

Día de los Muertos en Tepotzlán

In Tepotzlán, people celebrate the Day of the Dead instead of Halloween. This is when families remember their relatives who have died. According to *The Skeleton at the Feast*,[1] the Day of the Dead was probably celebrated before Europeans came to Mexico a little more than 500 years ago. The Aztecs believed that the dead spent eternity in a place determined by their mode of death. The most prestigious afterlife was accorded to men who died in war and women who died in childbirth.

The Day of the Dead is actually two days. November 1 is Día de los Niños, when children who have died are remembered. In Tepotzlán, where I visited in 1999 while researching a book, some customs have begun that resemble Halloween. For example, the children carve little squashes. They are about eight inches tall with white interiors and a thin green exterior that is much more forgiving to amateur carvers than the hard shell of the orange pumpkin.

❖ ❖ ❖ ❖ ❖

All that day, street vendors hawked the little squashes. In doorways and courtyards, I could see adults, usually a father, helping children carve the pumpkins. I noticed that the young woman who ran the Posada Alí, where I was staying, had a little sister who was usually with her. She was a sweet, bright little girl. Both of their parents, the older girl told me, worked, and were gone all the time. Since I had nowhere to be until later that night, I went out and bought a little pumpkin and began to carve it with my penknife. This is something I always do at home, as well, although with a better knife.

A family from Mexico City was also staying at the posada, and when the mother saw me on the back patio carving, she insisted that her husband get a pumpkin and carve it for their children. He reluctantly went out, and I soon saw him struggling with a pumpkin. I was carving a cat face, and it was turning out pretty well.

The children take off the tops and hollow them out, then carve designs in the sides. Instead of faces, however, they usually carve crosses. They poke a hole in the bottom and put the tip of a long candle in, letting most of the candle protrude from the bottom. They then put two holes in the sides near the top and run the ends of a short rope through it. When the candle is lit, the squash becomes a small lantern that the child can carry through the streets, holding it by the rope. As the candle burns down, they push it up from the bottom. If this sounds awkward, it is.

When I had finished carving the cat pumpkin, I set it on the front desk when no one was looking. In a few minutes, the older girl, who had been very cool to me when I checked in, came to ask if I had carved the pumpkin. She had earlier insisted on 600 pesos up front, and would not take a credit card or traveler's check. The bank would not cash my traveler's check on Saturday, and would not be open again until Tuesday, because Monday was a national holiday. Their ATM was locked behind an iron grill, far beyond my reach.

I admitted that I had left the lantern, and that it was for her little sister. The younger girl was ecstatic, because it meant she could go door-to-door, at least close by. I am not sure why their parents did not carve a pumpkin for them, or if the parents even existed.

As soon as it was dark, around seven in the evening, the children went from house to house through the narrow, uneven streets. Their mothers and fathers went with them. At each house, the children shouted, *"Almas para mi calabaza!"* which means, "Alms for my pumpkin!" Then people put candy in the plastic bags that the children were carrying. In the past, the almas, or charity, were in the form of small coins. But now it is usually candy. Because of the use of the word *almas*, I think the tradition may date from at least the nineteenth century, if not earlier.

Most of the local children were not in costume, but some wore white, belted sheets that resembled the dress of penitents. There is a distinct divide between the locals and the upper-class Mexicans who visit from the metropolitan area. The locals are very proud of their traditions and are trying to preserve them in the face of continuous change and development, and this is highlighted during the Day of the Dead festivities, when so many visitors come from out of town. Some of the children visiting from Mexico City wore store-bought, commercial costumes, such as Batman and little witches, and so, oddly, did some of their parents. The local children from Tepotzlán did not wear character costumes, either because of cost or tradition.

∴ ∴ ∴ ∴ ∴

November 2 is Día de los Muertos to remember the adults. On the night of November 2, the tall gates of the cemetery are opened, and people visit the graves of their families. They take flowers and candles and food, as well as soap, water, and tools to clean the gravestones, weed around them, and decorate the graves. Preparation for this may start weeks in advance.

The local produce market is filled with fresh flowers, dried flowers, and foodstuffs that people look through carefully, trying to choose only the best to use for their private celebrations. Little skulls are everywhere, formed out of either white sugar or a local candy made of seeds and honey. These can be inscribed across the forehead with your own name or the name of a deceased. These are often purchased and given to children, all in a spirit of fun and affection. There is the same air of bustle and festive enterprise that one feels in the United States on Christmas Eve.

The most important flower used during Day of the Dead is the marigold. The petals are scattered on the graves or at the entrances to houses to show the spirits they are welcome. Decorations are made out of the whole marigold flower. In some houses and churches, people build altars, or shrines, to remember the dead. In Nahuatl, the original language around Mexico City, the word for marigold is *sempasuchil.*

On the night of November 2, many families take a picnic to the cemetery. This is the one time of year when people are encouraged to think and talk about those whom they have lost, singing songs and telling stories about the dead. The rest of the year, families are not supposed to dwell on this sadness. Families may bring food or other things that had been favorites of the person who died. They may spend the entire night in the cemetery, in the company of many other families, or construct an altar at home.

The spirits, following the sempasuchil petals, return at midnight. A typical *ofrenda* is hot chocolate (or the spirit's favorite beverage), sweet baked bread, tamales, rice, and beans. Once an ofrenda has been made available to the spirits, the living are permitted to eat it. The spirits partake of only the "essence" of the food, but people claim that you can taste the difference — the food retains its nutritional value, but loses some of its flavor. After midnight, the family eats, and remembers through the act of eating the beloved departed.

Home altars have become popular in the United States, where people are far from their origins, and the altar has become an artistic expression of this longing for connection to something deeper. I now build one in my own home each year as a way to talk about my family to my son. I have a set of square baskets with lids, like boxes, that I can assemble into a small platform and backing to which photos and flowers can be pinned. I have tiny papier-mâché skeletons playing musical instruments and an elegant La Caterina, and tissue paper cutouts that can be draped around the edges. My husband also contributes a photo or memento now and then, which gives him an opportunity to talk about his family as well. Sometimes, we include former pets, like my husband's German Shepherd, Blue. Each year, we make it a little different, maybe honoring different ancestors or using new decorations.

In Seattle, our writers group, Los Norteños, has begun a tradition of a public reading and altar to which all are invited to contribute. From the first year we staged this at The Elliott Bay Book Company, around ten years ago, the reading has been packed with people from all backgrounds. We also collect donations for a local charity.

But the people of Tepotzlán and other traditional communities know that you need to be there in the flesh in order to close the circle of life and death with the ancestors, the land, and the living. At least, I felt, while I was in Tepotzlán, I had carved a pumpkin for a little girl. My visit to the pyramid the following day would show how much I belonged, or didn't belong, to this place.

Fandango

JOURNAL EXCERPT — NOVEMBER 2
The key to laundry is agitation.
I'm so glad I brought a suitcase I could carry. I never would have made it to Tepotzlán otherwise.

I visited Tepotzlán at the invitation of a writer and college instructor who lives there. She is a Mexican born of foreign parents. She married a Mexican, had three children ranging in ages from 10 to about 18, divorced about three years earlier, and moved to Tepotzlán because her husband "could never make up his mind about anything." Including, I presume, moving to Tepotzlán.

The instructor teaches literature at a college in Cuernavaca. She translated a collection of work by Chicana writers, *Las formas de nuestras voces: Chicana and Mexican Writers in Mexico*, into Spanish and had it published in Mexico. Bilingual Review Press distributed the anthology in the United States, which is how she knows the editor, my original connection.

She took me to a "fandango — *bailes hasta que mueres*" on October 31, a benefit for a local arts and artisans school. It was held in a courtyard on the grounds of the school. There was a 35-peso admission fee, plus food. Everything was wonderful. I had a *tamal* and a La Victoria, but was afraid to have more because I hardly had any pesos after paying for my room at La Posada Alí. The party was la crème de la crème de Tepotzlán, and everyone dressed up. My friend, who is blonde and blue-eyed, wore black velvet. Several of the artists had made an ofrenda, an offering for the Day of the Dead, which was quite beautiful. It had several tiers with candles, and cut-out paper designs in blue and yellow. On the ground were flat, colored sculptures in sand. In front of that, laid out on the ground, was the large valentine shape of a heart made entirely of whole marigold flowers. At first I thought part of the bottom had been shuffled out of line, then realized that it was a stylized bleeding heart. From the rafters over the whole hung tissue paper cut-outs in many colors.

After several phone calls saying that she would be a little late, during which time I purchased and carved the pumpkin, my friend arrived with two of her children to pick me up in her car. We arrived at the fandango about 9:30. Musicians were playing traditional Mexican music, and the guests were dancing on a small square of concrete on the school grounds. Both the musicians and dancers played and danced madly, as though they really would dance until they dropped.

The kitchen concession was set up under a ramada, and small tables and chairs were scattered around. It took some doing to gather enough chairs together with a table for our group to sit down.

I was introduced to an American and his Mexican girlfriend. The expat had been there ten years, spoke little Spanish, and told people he was an architect. He had built a house for his mother in Tepotzlán twenty years earlier and now lived there. He had been a blues musician in the United States for a while.

I think of him as a typical American expat, although I'm not sure why, since I haven't spent much time in Mexico, and didn't know any expats in Chihuahua whom I remember. As a fourteen-year-old, I remember visiting Ajijíc, a community of Americans near Lake Chapala, with my family and not liking it much. I remember old white people, seated in metal chairs near the edge of a swimming pool, reaching out to touch my arms and saying, "We don't see many young people around here." Except for the Mexicans, I remember thinking, who wait on you hand and foot while you criticize them as though they are not there. It might have been one of the first times I really sensed the rift between who I was and who these people saw as "human."

I think what bothered me about the American was that he made some comments about what life had come to in the United States, and how it wasn't worth supporting "the system" anymore, rhetoric that sounded about twenty-five years out of date. I translated this to mean that once his mother died, the man could afford to live in Mexico without working.

His girlfriend turned out to be much more interesting, working on a set of seminars planning for Mexico in the next century. Her father is a famous writer and intellectual who lives in a commune in Cuernavaca. She was interested in meeting some of the contacts I had made in Mexico City and said she would e-mail me more information on her own projects.

My friend, meanwhile, was downing shots of tequila and eating. It had been a long time, she said, since she had had time to celebrate. When the music switched to salsa, she got up to dance. Before going out to the dance floor, she introduced me to several people who didn't seem too interested in talking to me. My already-tenuous Spanish began to fail me as the night wore on.

Most of the people at the party seemed to be wealthy Mexico City residents who also maintain a residence in Tepotzlán. Because it is a relatively small town, 18,000, I think, some people prefer to raise their children there rather than in the city. All of the children over the age of ten seemed to be at the party, and they had the sort of maturity at that age that one doesn't usually see in the United States. All of those I spoke with attended the Preparatoria (college prep) school in Cuernavaca. Only the local, indigenous people send their children to the public schools.

We left the party at 12:30 because my friend's youngest daughter had fallen during the day at school and hurt her leg. She had wanted to go home all evening. Her other daughter and her boyfriend had taken the car, in the meantime, and it took awhile to find them and it on one of the nearby streets. My friend seemed to know where to look, so the daughter must have been at a specific location. I was willing to walk back to La Posada, since it wasn't that far, but she insisted on driving me. When we finally located the car, all six of us piled in.

"Didn't you say it was safe here?" I asked.

"Yes," she answered, "but wherever people have been drinking, you always need to be cautious."

With our loaded car, we maneuvered through the potholes of Tepotzlán to the other end of town. We passed the public basketball courts, where the rest of the town was having a party. This consisted of amplified "techno-disco" with a DJ, a couple of carnival rides, and plenty of beer and tequila. It is legal to drink on the streets of Tepotzlán, and many stands sell tequila by the shot or bottles of beer. Throngs of teenagers were standing around, as well as a few men who were visibly drunk.

The second party, which was near La Posada Alí, went on until almost 2:30 AM, the throb of the techno beat reverberating through the ancient stone streets and buildings.

Around 4, I woke to the sound of the dogs of Tepotzlán howling. I was shivering, the only time during my entire visit to Mexico that I was cold. I got up and put every blanket in the room on the bed and went back to sleep.

Climbing the Pyramid

The last thing my friend said to me on Saturday night was, "Climb the pyramid tomorrow morning. It takes about 45 minutes. Then call me."

I woke up about 7:00 feeling happy and well rested, although I had woken with chills a few hours earlier. The dogs had been howling and carrying on, their calls bouncing off the cliffs surrounding the town. But the morning light was clear and inviting. I realized that I had awakened each morning in Mexico City with feelings akin to a hangover from the bad air. I showered, dressed, and went out to pick up a *pan dulce* and juice for breakfast. Around 9:30 I walked uphill to the edge of Tepotzlán where the path to the pyramid began.

First there was a sign that said it was two kilometers to the pyramid. Not bad, I thought, about a mile. Then there was a sign that said something like there was a park fee of three pesos, no refunds, no matter what. I paid my three pesos and kept going. A bargain, I thought, to climb a real pyramid set in these beautiful mountains.

All the time, the cobblestone path had climbed uphill and gotten narrower and narrower. Food and trinket vendors were setting up their stalls for the day, Sunday, November 1, probably one of the biggest days of the year for them.

One or two vendors sold small carvings of wood, showing the pyramid in a rough-hewn setting that was supposed to represent the mountains. After the trail had given up any pretense of being a road, it got steeper and rougher. There were many family groups climbing, with *abuelas* and small children. We passed a stand that rented or sold carved wooden walking sticks.

That day, I saw a different kind of dog from those in town. It was just above the last concession stand, where the trail really began to get steep. I don't know if the dog had come up from the town or lived on the mountain. It was a smaller dog with a sharp muzzle and large ears. Most of the dogs in town were light tan in color and had long tails that curled over their backs. This dog looked just like those in the ancient paintings by the Mayas, or the little figurines of dogs one sometimes sees. It might have belonged to one of the concessionaires, but it seemed at home on the mountain in a way that I cannot explain. None of the dogs in town ever barked at or threatened people, and this one did not, either. But it seemed to be keeping an eye on those who were coming up the trail.

We began to climb. It was very humid, and I was soon exhausted. We were at about 6,500 feet in altitude. I had to stop and rest every fifteen minutes or so. Soon, I began to play a sort of relay race with some of the individuals and family groups—first one would progress, then stop while the other went forward. We would greet and encourage each other as we passed. It got steeper and steeper, and after about half an hour I asked a group coming down if we were almost there yet. They said not even halfway. The trail, now extremely rough, was a tumble of rocks and boulders that rose through forests of oak and elm. Flowering vines grew among them, and many of the flanking boulders were furry with moss.

At some point, I realized that we were climbing ancient carved stones, former parts of a former pyramid, now lying in a jumble on the ascent to the main pyramid. The trail grew narrower, and families had to wait while others squeezed past on the path. On one side was stone. On the other, air.

We squeezed through a narrow slot between two huge boulders, then the trail descended a bit to a stream that crossed the trail before plunging off the edge. I was really, truly exhausted, but knew I might as well finish the job since I had gotten this far. More people were coming back down the trail, those with an early start who had seen the pyramid and returned. Sempasuchil petals began to appear along the path. I thought I heard a conch shell trumpet a little later, but it might have been my imagination, since no one else seemed to notice.

The trail narrowed again and began a series of short switchbacks up a steep chute. The stones stopped at a steel ladder about twelve feet wide, which we climbed. I was careful to focus on the rungs and not on the rocky wasteland beneath. I hauled myself off of the top of the ladder, each expenditure of strength now calculated, measured — and onto another series of switchbacks.

At the top was a small building and an open patio-like area to the right. I staggered out to admire the view of Tepotzlán, flung out below us like a shawl on a bench. Only after my heart had slowed a bit did I realize that the pyramid was off to my right, where a group of teenagers encouraged a straggling friend from a ledge above us by chanting his name in unison: "Che-qué! Che-qué!"

The sempasuchil blossoms continued past where I sat. Soon a group of three men, a boy, and a woman came by, strewing more blossoms along the way and, yes, blowing a conch shell. I wondered if the local tourism bureau paid them to do this. They looked as though they didn't care about the rest of us, locals and tourists alike, however, and continued on to disappear around the far side of the pyramid. I got up and followed them.

The pyramid was surrounded by a sort of patio with amazing views in every direction. It was, without question, the real thing, although I had never seen one before outside of pictures in magazines. The sempasuchil petals continued up one side, which consisted of a series of short, steep stairs that had to be climbed with hands and feet. By now, the sun was harsh and bright. It was almost exactly noon. The pyramid itself offered almost no shelter, although people stood or sat around its base. A sign in English, Spanish, and Nahuatl offered a terse description, and a visitor was trying to read the Nahuatl out loud. It gave the estimated date of construction and told a little about the people who built it. But I was intent on following the living, so I continued on.

I clambered up to the top, where the teenagers sat with their legs dangling off the far edge, overlooking the approach. As I gained the top, I began to have a feeling of unease, and felt compelled to offer a prayer, perhaps to justify my trespass in this place.

But rather than saying Dear God as I normally would, I felt myself searching for a better term, a more appropriate form of address for the time and the place. I ended up praying, "Dear Mother of us all, dear Father of us all," with images of the moon and the sun in my head. The odd thing is, I can't remember what I prayed for. I said a complete prayer of some sort in my head, of thanks or a request or both, but I have been unable to recall what it was. There was a certain amount of fear in the act.

I found myself facing an area enclosed on three sides by a low wall. It was chained off on the near, open side. Inside of this enclosure, the group with the flowers had begun to set up an ofrenda. The group consisted of five people, an older woman, a teenage boy, and three men. Again, it struck me that they paid no attention to the crowd, neither smiling nor acknowledging anyone, nor offering any explanation of what they were doing. They were not dressed in colorful ceremonial clothing, although some people in town had been, but wore the clothes of the working poor—cotton trousers and skirts and rough, gray, woolen sweaters, probably made from local goat hair. They laid out whole sempasuchil blossoms one by one, and a small pile of sticks had been prepared as though to be lit at a later time. Every action was slow and deliberate.

It was hot and crowded, and the top of the pyramid was as unrelentingly uncomfortable as its sides. I felt like a bug on a hot plate in the sun. This was not a place intended to inspire a sense of well-being in humans, I realized. This was a place for the gods, and people were superfluous unless they had further business with the immortals. I did not, so I started down. As I rounded the base of the pyramid and walked down towards the first patio, I passed a small indentation I had not noticed before. Turning to look at it, I realized it was a stone cup intended to hold an offering, probably blood. It had been numbered as an archaeological artifact, but left in place. Seeing it reinforced my impression that it was time for me to leave. The experience, to me, had been in the journey.

A few years earlier, a Swiss company had tried to install a cable car that would have transported visitors from the town, up the steep slope, and directly to the top. The townspeople had opposed and successfully quashed the project. The same had happened with a proposed golf course and real estate development on another slope above the town. In that case, the project had actually broken ground when the women of Tepotzlán sat down in front of the bulldozers. When security guards tried to remove them, the men stepped out of the woods with rifles, saying, "I'm sorry, but my wife is a very stubborn woman. You see how she is. But if you harm her, I have no choice but to defend her." Shots were fired, and two of the locals were killed. But the development was put on hold, at least for now.

On the long, arduous climb up the mountainside, my lungs pleading for oxygen and my soft muscles protesting the unusually strenuous exercise, I thought about what a good idea a cable car would have been. I could have been up and back within an hour. Just think how much better it would be, I thought, for all these grandmas and young children struggling up the trail. But on the way back, my eyes and heart were full of moon and sun and sempasuchil petals. With each step I placed between myself and the pyramid, the better I felt.

Now that it was early afternoon, many more people were coming up the trail.

"How much farther is it?" someone asked.

"You are about halfway there," I said, "and it gets much worse."

If people want to see this place, I thought, let them walk. We are all pilgrims here. Let them walk.

∴ II ∴

On Family and Culture

When Do You Sing?

A few years ago, I visited family members in El Paso, Texas. Some were people I hadn't seen in ten years, since my last visit to an aunt in Chihuahua. Others, like my cousin Güera, I hadn't seen since I was very young. At the age of six, I had been a flower girl in her wedding. She was twenty-four at the time. I had kept the green lace fingerless gloves from that outfit for years, until I could no longer force my hands into them. Now I wish I had still kept them.

During this visit, we all sat in my Aunt Julieta's little apartment and ate. She has left her house in Chihuahua and now lives in what started as a Jewish retirement center in El Paso, where her two sons and their families live. There were beans and *nopalitos* and rice and tamales. There was a salad my cousin Joel had brought. There is always a lot of food when my family gets together.

My other aunt, Julia, who is Güera's mother, looked exactly the same as when I was little, except her hair is white now instead of black. She is the same age as my father, and moved to El Paso when her daughter and granddaughter did. She sat smiling on the couch, not talking too much, while Julieta bustled around fixing food in the tiny kitchen area and making sure everyone had more than enough to eat.

We talked about the church choir in which most of my cousins used to sing, at the Mexican Protestant church they attended in Los Angeles. My cousin Güera used to direct the choir with one hand and play the vibraphone with the other, holding two or three mallets in her fist, and had a powerful voice, which she added to the choir. She adored Lionel Hampton. Her daughter also used to sing—even as a child, an amazing duplicate of her mother. I asked if there were any recordings of the choir. She said no, the only one had been ruined by someone to whom they had loaned it.

I asked if she still sang. She looked very sorrowful. Over a year earlier, she'd had a stroke. She is not sure when, exactly. One day she was driving and realized that she couldn't see everything on the left, that the center line kept disappearing. She had to give up driving.

"Two months after I bought a new car," she said. "And there it sits in the garage."

She can't sing anymore, she said, because she can't control the pitch of her voice; the left half of her vocal cords are frozen, although it is not apparent in her speech.

"When do *you* sing?" she said to me.

The question surprised me. She asked it as though she could not imagine not singing, if one were able, and I realized how important it had been to her.

I really had to think. Both of my sisters have always been more musical. One sings at church and plays the piano, the other plays the guitar. I was only pulled in if they needed a third to sing alto or tenor. My mother, who gave piano lessons, taught me to read music, but that was about it.

My mother always had delusions of the perfect American family. She got this idea from watching the Lawrence Welk Show on television. There were three or four girls called The Lennon Sisters who dressed alike in fluffy outfits with matching bows in their hair and sang together. It is possible that she named me Kathleen after one of them. Because she couldn't talk anymore, also the victim of a stroke, I couldn't ask her.

I thought and thought. My house is full of my son's music. He plays the piano. He writes music and listens to CDs in his room, or in the living room when he can get away with it. There is no room for more music in the house.

"I sing in the car," I said finally. "I sing when I'm driving alone in the car."

Like my writing, it is something I mostly do when I am alone.

∴ ∴ ∴ ∴ ∴

A month later, my mother died. She had been confined to a nursing home for several years, no longer able to move or speak. Her death was a blessing.

My cousin Güera, her mother Julia, and her brother Mike, who lived in the Bay Area, were all too ill or frail to attend the funeral in Southern California. But my Aunt Julieta and her daughter, Priscila, were able to come from El Paso and Chihuahua, along with representatives of other branches of the family. We are all older now, and most of my cousins have grandchildren.

The funeral was to be held in a mortuary chapel in Riverside, California, where my father had prepaid for mortuary and funeral services. Nevertheless, there are a lot of details to planning a funeral, just like a wedding, except with less notice.

My middle sister, it turned out, has a lot of experience planning funerals. "Everyone is so old in North Dakota," she said, "that we have funerals all the time."

She engaged a Spanish-speaking pastor who knew my parents. This was a relief to me, because I was afraid that my father, who is also ordained as a Methodist minister, would try to conduct the service himself. The pastor, in turn, brought a pianist to accompany us during the two hymns my sisters had picked out. There were flowers delivered at the last minute before 10:00 AM, and little buff-colored programs. My son was able to fulfill a lifelong dream to ride in a limousine. It glided, large and white and sharklike, from my parents' house in Grand Terrace along Interstate 10, which had been closed the day before due to a spill of hydrochloric acid from a train. When we arrived at the airport from Seattle, it had taken us two hours to drive from Ontario to San Bernardino along the back roads. The day of the funeral, there was no sign of the deadly chlorine gas generated by the spill. The sun shone in that artificial way that it shines in Southern California, a little gray from the smog, a little muted, but hot and steady.

During the funeral, my son and I sat in the front row so that my father would not be alone, with my two sisters and their families directly behind us. Earlier, I had grabbed a box of tissue and placed it next to my father, praying that all would go smoothly. After some waiting, we asked that the piped-in music be turned down, and my ten-year-old son plinked out "Gavotte in D" by Bach on a decrepit Yamaha keyboard as a prelude to the service. Later, he told me that the only setting on which it would play was guitar.

My cousin Paul was asked to deliver the eulogy. He talked about my mother's devotion to music, and how that had been so much a part of our family's communal life and identity. I don't think of him as an overly emotional man, but he broke down as he spoke. I knew that he was thinking about his own mother, who had died a year earlier. On her way to lunch in a restaurant to celebrate her birthday, accompanied by two of her granddaughters, my Aunt Arcelia had refused assistance down an uneven path. She had fallen head forward over her walker and broken her neck. In the hospital, pinned into a metallic halo to keep her neck in place, she had asked to be released. My cousin watched a last sunset with her before she died.

After the eulogy and an emotional tribute from my father, my sister's nineteen-year-old son stood and made a long, rambling statement. My oldest sister and her two children had lived with my parents for the last ten years, so the children were close to my mother. I knew this tribute was at his sister's behest, who was in Spain as a missionary. Also at her bidding, he was videotaping from the back of the room during the service. This bothered me, since the point of a funeral seemed lost after the fact, but I was thankful that he was not lying in the aisle on his stomach taping, or crab-walking around in front.

As we stood to sing a hymn, the accompanist proceeded to the keyboard, holding the sheet music supplied by my sisters. A few faltering notes were sounded of what was supposed to be "Jesus Is All the World to Me," before we realized that he could not play the melody. It is possible that he could not read music, and the hymn, a favorite of my mother's, was unfamiliar to him. Some people play only by ear. The person who normally would have taken over at this point was my mother. We needed my mother to play the piano at her own funeral.

All of this time, I had carefully avoided the front of the chapel. I had stayed away from it before the service, and had sat in front only reluctantly, so that my father would not be by himself. My sisters and their families sat behind us. This is because I did not wish to see and remember my mother in her last, deteriorated state. As she had lain in a nursing home over the years, her ability to move slowly diminishing until she could not even speak, her body had slowly lost its shape, until it had seemed vast and amorphous. But when we stood to sing, I accidentally glanced into the open casket. Before I could avert my eyes, I noted a slash of dark red lipstick on her lips, and a stretch of pink, pleated material over her distended abdomen. I wondered if it was really a dress or if the mortuary had fashioned a covering that mimicked regular clothing. I doubted that any of her own dresses fit her anymore.

After a moment or two of listening to the pianist fumble with the keyboard, one voice began a cappella, and the rest of us joined in. We sang the first verse in unison, then broke into harmony for the following verses. We sang in a strong, clear voice, the Mexican way. People in Anglo churches sing politely, even timidly, as though afraid to offend. We make our voices as strong as possible, as though trying to cut through the noise of everyone else on the planet. Even my son, sensing that this was important, joined in, although singing hymns in Spanish can be tricky, involving more than one syllable per note.

When we sing all together, something primal is created, something having to do with the sound that closely related people make. The veneer of the hymn form stretches thin, sounding like a cross between a Maori missionary choir and Welsh coal miners. We made a deep, booming sound that filled the room and spilled out into the building and air beyond, emanating out into the quiet Saturday morning of the run-down neighborhood. I could feel the clamp inside of my chest loosen slightly, as it made way for the air going in and out of my lungs, as I added my voice to that sound that was so familiar, yet only existed when we were all together.

Later, I recalled a story I had heard on the radio. In 1999, the San Antonio Vocal Arts Ensemble, or SAVAE, premiered a performance of ancient Aztec chant, re-created from a written fragment. This was a form that, according to one of the members, existed long before the Spanish Conquest, with chants that were particular to each region and village. But when the Catholic priests brought European chants, they were quickly memorized and taken back to the villages. Like imported weeds growing up through the cracks of history, the new chants soon replaced the traditional.

More recently, scientists have begun to explore the purpose of singing. Why do we sing? I think I know the answer. To sing is to recognize your clan. I am sure that on the ancient hills and plains, voices were raised to call and recognize the other across the field, the forest — other, but the same. And when we sing together, we confirm that kinship — a sameness that transcends the boundaries of language and occupation and other disparities that exist even within families.

That's how it feels when our family sings, as though it supercedes our known history. It ties us together in a way that conversation and even food do not.

By the time we got to that last hymn, "¡Cuán Grande es El!"[1] the accompanist might as well have gone home. Like wolves howling across the darkling plain, we filled that sunny Saturday morning with a confirmation of our bond. In one last tribute to my mother, an act of catharsis through our sorrow, we raised our voices and sang.

My Mother's Vase

For the second time in five years, I found myself standing in my front doorway, waiting for the earth to stop heaving around. I wondered about the safety of my son at school, and peered up the road to see if the neighbors' homes were standing.

Each time, I found myself clutching an old *jarra*, a water jar, that my parents bought long ago in Mexico. It is probably forty or fifty years old.

Why, I have to ask myself, of all the things in my house that I could grab on the way out, do I end up holding this jar each time? It is the color of loamy soil, with a lid that fits over the top that can double as a drinking glass. While I doubt that it was ever meant to be more than decorative, it is patterned on the jars that people used to keep in their homes to store fresh water. All the way around it is painted an idyllic scene from nature of deer and birds and *nopales*. It has a distinct pattern of crosshatching in the background that marks this particular style of pottery as being from a certain part of Mexico — Tonalá, I think, although I always forget. I suppose if I kept it for its resale value, I would know this.

I grew up in earthquake country, directly over the San Andreas fault in the mountains of San Bernardino. There was a sharp drop about midpoint in the pasture behind the Optimist Boys' Ranch, where my father was the superintendent, and we experienced small quakes on a weekly basis. As a result, I was fairly blasé about quakes, casually holding onto a doorway with one hand while continuing to read with the other. A favorite family story is that I slept through a major quake while we were visiting Mexico City in 1957. My mother and aunt were clinging to each other in terror while my father was down the hall trying to convince people not to run outside, where they might be killed by falling masonry. They later thanked him for saving their lives. Why should I worry? I had been told many times that it would pass.

But my second large quake on Bainbridge Island, the fourth since moving to the Northwest, sends me outside with an old vase. Shouldn't I try to save my computer? Or my wallet, in case I have to prove who I am to collect my son? How about the guitar, the one that has survived so many disasters in the past, including a brick-and-board bookcase collapsing on it in college? It's from Mexico, too.

Once it's over, I go back inside to check out the damage. This time, I'm sure there has to be some — I heard things falling. Miraculously, nothing is broken, and the light fixture over the dining room table has not ripped loose from its flimsy anchor, the one we keep meaning to fix. Although we are asked not to, I cannot refrain from calling my son's school, where I receive a busy signal. No surprise there. As it turns out, we can barely get a line off the island for the next several days, as calls flood in from friends and relatives from Alaska to Texas checking on our well-being. We're fine, we say. We send out a generic e-mail of reassurance and ask people to share it with others. No one was killed, *gracias a Dios*.

Since my days as a child when all I had to worry about was my own self-preservation, I have to admit that my attitude towards earthquakes has changed. Had the quake occurred on Tuesday, my son would have been at Boeing field participating in a simulation of a *Challenger* mission. His team-teaching class was there on Wednesday, the day of the quake, and the children were impressed with the realism of the emergency situation that developed. Staff and volunteers quickly roped off areas where there was broken glass and made it a positive experience for the students.

I resisted going to school, since the community grapevine had already informed me that there had been no structural damage on Bainbridge. My son, Ben, returned home on the bus, where more parents than usual waited at our stop. We were cool, but not that cool. Ben, on the other hand, declared that he had been in the most earthquake-proof building on the island, the new Sakai Intermediate School, opened a year ago. Still, I thought, I would have preferred to have it tested once without him in it.

The vase is back on its shelf in the dining room, on an old bookcase, where it completes the Arts and Crafts look of our house.

I think I took it because it is old, it is easily portable, and it represents everything that I cannot grab and hold onto as things change around me — my son, my youth, my fragile relationships with other people. If it falls, it will hit bare floor and break. But there is no safe place, not really, in a world that is full of random movement.

Vipiniguat-Ru

Great-Grandmother, Deceased

This is the story of an obsession. It is the story of looking for something that is probably not there, yet the urge to search persists, like an old song stuck in your head, or the memory of an amputated hand.

This is the story of my search for my maternal grandmother's story, and the story of her mother as well. It is the willing of the spirit to raise old bones, to connect old images, uncover rumors and histories that have been carefully covered up and forgotten.

My grandmother was the daughter of an Opata woman and an Irish father. As part of a novel, *The Flower in the Skull*,[1] I wrote a story that I thought might be very much like hers. For lack of concrete information, I concocted her story as part of a larger historical fiction set along the border, real or imagined, between the United States and Mexico. It goes like this:

Rosa's Story

My mother brought me into the world when she was fourteen years old, barely a woman, in pain, in sorrow, and in deep humiliation.

I was born in Nogales, Arizona, where my mother and her mother's family had gone to live after the soldiers destroyed their home in the Sonoran Desert, about one hundred miles farther south. My mother was an Opata Indian, and the policy of the Mexican government was to break up the Indian settlements, scatter the families, and obliterate their way of life. That way, there were fewer local governing councils to give trouble. The Mexican government has always found local government to be inconvenient.

The Opatas, on the other hand, had never been conquered.

Long known for their bravery, even the women had slain con-
quistadors in hand-to-hand combat. If necessary, the women
had allowed the Spaniards to take them into their quarters and
undress them. When the men in turn undressed, the Opata
women seized their discarded swords and rammed them into the
soldiers' bellies. They were willing, as individuals, to die in
order to save the culture.

But this did not work. Every twenty or thirty years, new
soldiers returned, and more of them, until an Opata chief made
a truce with them: the Opatas would fight with the Spanish, if
the soldiers would help to fight against the Apaches, the plague
from the north. The Opata chief was made a general of the
nation by the commandant general of the Interior Provinces.
This worked for awhile; the Spanish soldiers by now admired
the Opata very much for their courage and ferocity, but in the
end, over the generations, this would not bring peace.

In 1884 the soldiers came again and burned down my
mother's village. They shot and killed many of the people, doing
terrible things to all the young girls they could catch. The people
knew that the governor of Sonora would do nothing, could do
nothing, for he was as afraid of the soldiers as they were. Those
who could escaped, and some came to live with relatives in
Nogales, where many of the Pimas had already settled in order
to escape the constant bloodshed.

We have known the Pimas for a long time, and many of our
people have married them and lived in their villages. The soldiers have never liked them, either, because they too, are a proud
people.

My mother Pastora came to Nogales and her family was very
poor. They had nothing to eat. Pastora was tall and strong, like
her father and her uncles, and she was sent to work in the house
of a rich family in the city. They were happy to have her.

There was a family in town of red-headed people, from Ire-
land. They had a son who wanted my mother, Pastora, to go
with him and let him have his way with her, but she refused.
People thought that just because they were Indians, they would
do anything.

And so, one Sunday afternoon, when no one else was at
home, he came into the house where she worked. He must have

watched the house to know that the people she worked for were gone. He came into the house, and against her will, he used her. He raped her. And then he left.

She was afraid to leave the house, since she lived there now, but she ran away and went to find her mother's family. She told her mother what happened. And she refused to go back to that house.

When the people returned, they did not know what had happened to my mother, Pastora. They waited for her to return, angry that she had left the house unlocked, then worried that she did not return. They liked my mother very much.

Finally, after several days had passed, the man of the house went to the Indian settlement, where my mother's family lived, and found my mother with them. My grandmother told him what had happened, and said that she could not allow her daughter to return. The man asked who had done it. When my mother told him, he could not believe that it was the son from the red-headed family. He thought she was lying. The man returned to town without my mother.

At home, the man told his wife, and the wife, who loved my mother and wanted her back to take care of her children, went to the red-headed Irish family and told them what Pastora had said. To everyone's surprise, the young man, who was hardly older than my mother, about eighteen, confessed. He said that he loved my mother, and wanted to marry her.

The man who employed my mother went back to the Indian settlement and told my mother that George Voughan, for that was his name, wanted to marry her. She refused. She said that she never wanted to see him again in her life, or leave her family. The man returned to town with her answer.

George Voughan was very unhappy, but his mother was even more so, for she was very religious, and her son had shamed them. The family where my mother Pastora had worked was very unhappy as well, for they had been friends with the red-headed family, which was how George Voughan knew my mother. My mother was very unhappy, for she found that she could not bleed, because she was pregnant.

The white family who loved my mother found out that she was pregnant, and again, the wife sent her husband to the Indian settlement, which was by now getting used to seeing this man. The man came to my mother's family, and said that they would take care of my mother Pastora and her baby if she would only come back and live with them. She could take care of her own baby as well as theirs, and she didn't have to marry George Voughan if she didn't want to.

This seemed to suit the family, although my mother did not wish to go back. She was afraid of George Voughan. But her own family was very poor, and here she was about to bring another mouth into the world to feed. The family had no land of its own, no village, but lived with the Pimas who had escaped from Mexico.

So my mother Pastora went back to the house in town. The family was true to its word, and took my mother back to help them, and raise their babies, and clean their house. And so I was born in that house, in the city of Nogales, and was told that if a red-headed man ever tried to talk to me, to run away. For they were afraid that he would try to steal me. He never did.

∴ ∴ ∴ ∴ ∴

My mother was very beautiful, and the family had many friends, and one of them was a doctor named Dr. Martinez. He loved my mother and asked her to marry him, even though she already had me. And my mother loved him, because he seemed to be kind, and she wanted a house of her own, and so she married him. Her family was very happy, for things were hard for them.

Dr. Martinez gave me his name, made me his daughter, and we were very happy in that house. He was kind to me. But something terrible happened.

My mother was unable to have other children after me. Although Dr. Martinez gave her medicines to make her fertile, and her own mother gave her medicines to make her fertile, my mother Pastora was unable to conceive again. Her mother felt that she may have suffered some damage from what George Voughan did to her that Sunday afternoon, though no one really knew what had happened, only Pastora.

And so, something else terrible happened to my mother. Dr. Martinez left her for a woman whom he thought could give him children. He gave my mother some money, and found her a place to live, but he went to live with someone else, right there in town. I was about twelve years old. My mother was very sad, for she had loved Dr. Martinez, and I had thought he was my father. I did not understand the difference between a real father and a stepfather, I only knew that my mother had been happy, and so had I.

Now we were very poor. My mother's family could not take us back, but we had a place to live, and once in a while Dr. Martinez gave us some money. I went to work cleaning people's houses, for my mother was very sick. She missed her husband, and could think of nothing else, night and day; she could not sleep or eat. My mother, who had been beautiful and full of life, withered away before my eyes into an old woman.

When I was fourteen years old, I met a young minister who had come to Nogales to introduce people to his personal savior, Jesus Christ. I went with a friend to his church, and the people were very kind. They served food after the service, and talked about how much God loved us. They gave us pamphlets to take with us and read, and I took one, although I could only read a little bit.

I returned to the church whenever I could after that, because I liked the young minister. His name was Miguel Narro. After a few months, he asked to marry me. I told him he would have to obtain permission from my mother.

Miguel came to the house, and was kind to my mother. He seemed to be used to coming into poor people's homes. My mother liked him immediately, and gave us permission to marry. And so, on my fifteenth birthday, we did, and my mother was happy to see me married. But she was very sick, and died shortly afterwards. She never recovered from the way that Dr. Martinez had treated her, or, I guess, from George Voughan. My mother, Pastora Curiel Martinez, was not yet thirty years old when she died.

∴ ∴ ∴ ∴ ∴

As I wrote "Rosa's Story," I felt that I ought to take the time, eventually, to find out more about the Opata. The word haunted me, for although I had known we were part Indian, I was an adult and a mother before I learned the name of our tribe from a cousin in Chihuahua, Mexico. Much had been made of the Irish, but little of the Indian. So, spurred by my son's interest in our Native American heritage, I set out to find what I could find.

My initial search was not heartening. The Opata show up on older maps of the Southwest, one by the National Geographic published in 1976, one published in 1992 in *Ms.* magazine, to my delight. But I wasn't able to locate information on the tribe, and at first attributed it to the border, which was laid like a scar across the Southwest: tribes north of the border have been studied and documented, tribes south were mostly ignored.

Franciscans swept through the area, imposing their own view of heaven on earth, followed by the Jesuits, who took copious notes on the people they encountered. Father Kino wrote about the Opata, that they were brave, that they treated their women well, that they grew cotton and wove material. The main interest the Spanish had in the Opata was that they hated the Apaches, and so became allies with the Spanish in defending the northern frontier. Of course, the Apaches wouldn't have become a problem if the Spaniards had not disrupted their trade routes and supplied them with horses, but that's another story.

The Opata might have numbered approximately 60,000 at the time of the Conquest, and several dialects exist of their language. In other words, this tribe, whose name I did not know until 1990, numbered more than all the Pueblo peoples combined.

There is a big gap in the information, followed by American anthropologists and explorers taking their new religion, science, into the Opateria. In 1896, Carl Lumholtz led an expedition into Mexico in search of "primitive" people. His main goal was to contact and document the Tarahumara of the Sierra Occidental. This was post-Darwin, and people looked with fascination upon "primitives" as living relics of how their, that is, European, ancestors might have lived before they became "civilized." Lumholtz made a career of finding such people, authoring books such as *Among Cannibals*,[2] about his experiences in New Guinea. His book *Unknown Mexico*[3] is a study in dichotomy, where his documentation of highly complex cultures clashes with his own mindset that they were "primitive" people. In any case, Lumholtz got to Mexico and promptly fired most of his American help to hire native Mexicans, many of whom seem to have been of Opata descent.

"This territory (south of Nogales)," he writes, "was once in the possession of the large tribe of Opata Indians, who are now civilized. They have lost their language, religion and traditions, dress like the Mexicans, and in appearance are in no way distinguishable from the labouring class of Mexico with which they are thoroughly merged through frequent intermarriages."[4]

And yet, he adds a note at the end of his preface to the book: "Dr. Aleš Hrdlička, who has just returned from the Hyde expedition, informs me that in visiting the western part of Sonora he found pure Opata spoken west of Rio de Sonora and north of Ures, e.g., in Tuape."[5]

Nothing for several decades, then a series on anthropology published by the University of New Mexico in 1950 covering several Southwest tribes. Number six is *The Opata: An Inland Tribe of Sonora*,[6] by Jean B. Johnson. The paper was published posthumously by the widow, Mrs. Irmgard Weitlauer Johnson, who accompanied Mr. Johnson to Tónichi, Sonora, in 1940. The editor expresses some reservations about Mr. Johnson's linguistic findings, and the paper feels abbreviated, as though the author intended to say more at some points.

"The Opata," Johnson begins, "a group numbering some 60,000 at the time of the Conquest, have completely disappeared today as a cultural and ethnic identity. It is doubtful whether five persons could now be found who can recall even fragments of the language."[7]

If that was the case, what was Johnson doing in Sonora? He read the same material as everyone else, almost all of it written in the 1700s, then went to Sonora to document the Opata by inference from tribes that were not yet extinct, including the Cáhita (modern Yaqui-Mayo), the Yaqui, and the Lower Pima. It's a scant book, about fifty pages long, including long lists of vocabulary words taken, again, from earlier sources. It's the only publication I have found so far devoted exclusively to the Opata.

Why did I bother? Why learn about a people who no longer existed, and who seem to have willingly given up their separate identity to become, simply, Mexican?

In part it had to do with visiting the Anasazi ruins of the Four

Corners region. My son, first as an infant, then three, then four, would stand next to the crumbling walls, or view exquisite pottery, and say, "But where did they go?"

When I lived in Colorado from 1979 to 1983, the stock answer was: Nobody knows. They vanished mysteriously around 1100 BC. I went so far as to write a science fiction story portraying the Anasazi as space travelers who moved on to exploit natural resources elsewhere.

Now, the Pueblo people will tell you, "They were our ancestors. *We* are the Anasazi. But we call them Puebloans."

And so I tell my son, "They moved into houses with air conditioning. They became modern people, like us. And they live in the pueblos in New Mexico and Arizona."

Like us. And who are we? Well, we're part Opata. Are we extinct? Not exactly. I never made a big deal about being part Native American because I had never known much about it. After all, my parents are from Mexico, and almost all Mexicans are part Indian. Our culture and language are a blend of Indian and Spanish, one laid over the other. Perhaps the Opata culture is extinct, although I'm not entirely convinced of that. As little as I know about her, my great-grandmother, Pastora, identified herself as an Opata at the end of the nineteenth century in Nogales, Arizona. That implies that a context existed in which that would mean something. But it also raises some questions that might be of broader interest:

The Mexican government had a specific policy, beginning with its independence from Spain in 1840, of not recognizing Indian tribes. The official line was that "we are all Mexican, and so will be treated equally." This was, in part, to erase class distinctions and property rights that favored those born in Spain. The reality was that Indian rights were systematically violated, with deeds to land inevitably ending up in the hands of non-Indians. Strong local governments, especially Indian, were viewed with paranoia by the fledgling national government, and tribes that persisted in showing local strength and organization were attacked by federal troops. The Yaquis, for example, were killed, driven north, or sold into slavery to work on the henequen plantations in the Yucatán.

As a result of their conflict with the Mexican government, the Yaqui maintained a strong tribal identity. Rather than destroying them, it served to strengthen their traditions, ceremonies and lines of power, which had evolved after contact with the Jesuits into a unique culture of war and religion. Edward H. Spicer[8] and others have documented the Yaqui, who are still a living, vibrant people.

The Opata, on the other hand, were consistently praised for their bravery and compliance with the Spanish, then Mexican, government. In early encounters, the Opata resisted the Spanish invaders, the women going so far as to seduce the soldiers, then waiting until they set aside their arms before killing them with their own swords.[9] Once it was clear, however, that the soldiers were willing to kill Apaches, an alliance was quickly formed. The Opata were also quick to adopt European-style clothes, Christianity (in parallel with an indigenous belief system), and a town-centered, nonmigratory life, since they were primarily an agricultural society before the Conquest. All of these things led to more rapid acculturation than with other tribes.

Here we get a picture of "good" Indians and "bad" Indians, from the point of view of the Mexican government (obviously, as my Yakima friend pointed out, it would be the reverse from the Indian point of view). "Bad" Indians resist acculturation and spend a lot of time fighting, but maintain a distinct cultural identity and way of life; "good" Indians get absorbed, leaving merely a faded grease spot on the historical annals of the Southwest. When we look at recent events in Chiapas, we can see that Mexico's policy towards her indigenous people has not altered much in the hundred and fifty years since independence from Spain.

My great-grandmother was an Opata. Does that mean I am? I wasn't raised with any of the culture of the Opata. I was raised as a middle-class Mexican American in Southern California. I now live in the Northwest. The first and greatest loss of culture occurs when a people are separated from the land that sustains them. That land, with its plants, its soil, its water sources, sacred places, and the details of its climate and landmarks, is a notebook, a talking stick, that documents the stories of indigenous cultures. It is the frame upon which a culture is hung. Separated from that land, the details fall apart, become confused and blurry, and eventually lost.

In our case, this separation was due to the Mexican Revolution, but the Revolution was the culmination of hundreds of years of imbalance, of uprooting, of separating millions of people from their land.

When we look at this question from an American point of view, we get into this blood quantum issue that has both saved and defeated people. Assuming Pastora was full-blood, I'm one-eighth Opata. That is enough for membership in some tribes within the boundaries of the United States, but since my tribe doesn't seem to exist, and there isn't any economic incentive to being a member, it hasn't been a pressing issue. But there might be cultural reasons if, by chance, there are others like me, and just enough of a knowledge base left to preserve and at least aggregate the remnants of our culture.

Maybe it's like tree frogs in the Amazon: It's just one culture, but maybe the knowledge of the Sonoran Desert, of weaving and singing, of fighting and kinship patterns, contains some element that is crucial to the development of the human race as a whole.

I intend to keep reading the old scholarly texts, as well as a few newer ones that interpret old data with a modern sensibility. Ramón A. Gutiérrez has written a brilliant book, *When Jesus Came, the Corn Mothers Went Away*,[10] on the coming together of the Pueblo people and the Spanish in New Mexico. Gary Paul Nabhan, an ethnobotanist, works in the desert gathering seeds and stories that shed light on our culture, our health, and the future of our environment.[11] Campbell W. Pennington, a physical anthropologist, made extensive notes on the Opata that were never published.[12]

I suspect that whatever I write about the Opata will become somewhat definitive, since there's so little on them, so I feel a certain obligation to get things right. In reading all of this history, I find that each text is heavily colored by the background and expectations of the historian. In other words, history is an act of the imagination. Maybe this is why I write fiction. If there are larger truths to be known, perhaps they can only be discovered, delineated, if freed from the context of empiricism, another nineteenth-century idea that has shaped modern scholarship.

I'm not particularly interested in "the truth" about my great-grandmother, any more than the specifics of my grandfather's parents served as more than a catalyst for the writing of *Spirits of the Ordinary*.[13] She was born, she lived a hard life, and she died. I'm much more interested in discovering the forces of history that placed her in that time and place, and how an individual's world view evolved as society changed from a traditional one to a "modern" one. In other words, my goal is to create situations that can only be inferred from historical information. And I want my readers to connect with these situations on a level beyond that of shared history or bloodlines, to say, "Yes, I understand that, I feel what that woman felt." Admittedly, I read this history with feelings of poignancy, a certain sadness and nostalgia, that must come from my personal connection to it. But when I turn to writing, I know that original characters will spring from the page, ready to live out their lives regardless of what my ancestors may have done. Fiction is the act of rearranging history so that it has a narrative line, a story, a beginning, a middle, and, sometimes, a resolution. It seeks to capture truths that cannot be contained within the parameters of unadorned facts.

The paradox is that these universal truths, which is probably what Joseph Campbell would call them, can only be conveyed through specifics. In other words, the larger, the more inclusive, the more profound a truth is, the smaller the event we must use to convey that truth. And to find these specific moments in time—a young Opata catching a girl by the left nipple and leading her into the village to be his wife; keeping vigil with a comadre struck by lightning, lest her soul be unable to find its way back[14]—we must study history. And so fiction writers must rely on historians, scientists, journalists, cooks and dressmakers, preachers and nurses, newspapermen, dreamers, and people up to no good to supply us with the endless minutiae it takes to compose a story. The fabric of history provides us with our narrative threads.

Sooner or later, as I try to reimagine cultures and people, give them names and lives, I realize that I am going to have to spend some time in the Sonoran Desert, the Opateria. Books won't be enough. Maps won't do it. Even talking to people who know a lot will not be the same. I must see for myself what the Opata must have seen, even if I can never know or imagine a fraction of what they must have known.

More about My Great-Grandmother
and the Opata

I

My first book, *Mrs. Vargas and the Dead Naturalist*, is a collection based on the stories the older women in my family used to tell, and it is also based on my observations of them. It reflects, in part, the losses and gains of a generation cut off from their homeland by the Mexican Revolution, but is mostly about their interior lives. What are these carefully constructed women really like, I wanted to know. I have seen them all of my life in churches, in crowded living rooms, across tables laden with food. I have seen them in unguarded moments, gazing off into the middle distance. I wondered about their dreams and expectations, after all of the changes they had seen.

My second book, *Spirits of the Ordinary*, is about a man trying to find his place in the universe, a man whose parents are hidden Jews, yet who is drawn to the more dangerous aspects of life along the frontier — mining, loose women, and Indians. The last chapter of the book is told through the voice of his son, Gabriel, who marries a woman much like my grandmother, Rosaura Martinez. I made some attempts to research her tribe, the Opata, but didn't meet with much success, so I decided that I had to go to Arizona to find out more about them. This provided the basis for my third book, *The Flower in the Skull*.

The opportunity arose when I was a resident scholar at the Amerind Foundation outside of Tucson, Arizona. The Amerind has an extensive collection on the indigenous cultures of the Southwest, and the curator of collections, Allan McIntyre, was ready for me when I arrived. I spent hours going through this material and kept coming to some odd dead ends. Research was always done on people "like" the Opata, or descended from the Opata, yet there were no indications that the Opata were extinct, just that they didn't seem to be readily available to researchers.

Often, if I needed another book, Allan would go to the third floor of the library to get it for me. The library was one of two air-conditioned buildings in the compound, and an ancient body of indeterminate tribal affiliation was being stored there until it could be turned over to the appropriate people. Out of respect for the body, I was not allowed to use that floor of the library.

Eventually, I started calling anthropologists, then calling the people they recommended. The people I talked to kept getting older and older, and started passing messages on to each other — "If so-and-so is alive, give him my regards," or, "Tell him I've still got his photos." I even talked to Roz Spicer, who, with her husband, Edward, author of *Cycles of Conquest*, spent years among the Yaqui. I later discovered that her children had been raised with the help of an Opata nanny, who was still alive somewhere, but I did not meet her.

∴ ∴ ∴ ∴ ∴

At one point, a retired park service employee said there might be information about the Opata in reports on the restoration of a mission in Tumacacori, just north of Nogales. I read several of these reports, which detail the history, physical state, and reconstruction of the mission, which was originally built in 1691, abandoned once, repossessed by the Spanish missionaries, and finally abandoned to the Americans. There have been rumors of buried treasure for years, due to speculation that the priests buried their altarpieces before the first abandonment, or that there was a silver mine under it. At the bottom of the back page of one report, I found the following: "My friend Manuel Contreras, born in Cucurpe of Opata heritage, veteran of Chennault's Flying Tigers in China, and protector of Tumacacori for twenty years, personifies the contents of this booklet, which is dedicated to him."[1]

And then it struck me: The Opata were everywhere. They were the Mexicans who had moved north from the Sonoran Desert and provided the raw labor for Americans for the last 100 years. These were the people who were hauling lumber and mixing adobe and herding cattle and turning Tucson from an armed camp into a modern city.

I began looking more closely at material I had passed over. A monograph about the Marobavi, a group I had dismissed as being even more obscure than the Opata, since I had only come across the one mention of them, turned out to be a report about the Opata: the researcher, Roger Owen, had disguised the names and locations of the villages he visited, at the request of the people themselves.[2] A companion report by Thomas Hinton was a survey of Opata villages in northwestern Mexico.[3] By comparing the maps in the two reports, I was able to figure out which villages were covered in the Marobavi report.

I also discovered that Hinton had left extensive field notes and photographs at the Arizona State Museum that had never been published. The afternoon before I left I found an interview with the last known speaker of the Opata language, Juan Felipe Mayve, conducted in 1954 in Spanish. I didn't have time to read the interview, but I felt like the last surviving member of the family at the end of *One Hundred Years of Solitude*, by Gabriel García Márquez, reading his family's history as the house is burning down around him. I could not make a copy of the interview, but, because of archival restrictions on the material, had to have it made for me. When I received and read it weeks later, I found that it was the simple story of a man who was retired and lived with his daughter. He had worked hard all of his life. He remembered some of the language, but had not spoken it in a long time.[4]

After three weeks of research, I concluded that the Opata were one of the largest groups of people in the Southwest prior to the Conquest; that they were one of the least-researched groups; that their fate was tied to that of surrounding groups, such as the Apache and the Yaqui; and that few people today are willing to identify themselves as Opata. In fact, time after time, people who were thought of as Opata by their neighbors consistently denied it to outsiders, and refused to speak the language to them.

I struggled to understand how this could happen. How could such a big group, perhaps as many as 60,000 at the time of the Conquest, as many as all the Pueblo peoples combined, be reduced to this state? This may be due to several factors: the policy of the Mexican government towards indigenous people in Mexico, and how that changed at the end of the 1800s; The value of the land occupied by the Opata, which was rich farmland along the rivers of

Sonora; and the population pressures from the north, which forced the Apache farther and farther south until they were devastating the lands occupied by the Opata.

I have many unanswered questions. Primary among them is why similar pressures on groups such as the Yaqui strengthened their cultural identity, while weakening those of the Opata.

I found myself getting angry with the researchers whose work I was reading. Why, I wanted to know, didn't they write down more of the stories of these people, instead of just counting them? There is evidence that the Opata once occupied much of Southern Arizona — the place-names, such as Chiricahua, are in the Opata language. The folktales of the Opata line up with recent theories on migration, and there is evidence that they are an offshoot of the Pueblo peoples who just kept heading farther south.[5]

They may have been the people who built Casas Grandes, an ancient city in the state of Chihuahua similar to Mesa Verde. It produced a pottery style, Mata Ortiz, which has recently been revived by Juan Quezada, a non-Opata who understood its amazing beauty, and is being crafted and widely marketed today. All over Opata country are stone terraces and aqueducts that use the same engineering skills as those evident at Casas Grandes. How could people who had the ability to preserve at least remnants of this culture in an academic context have let it pass without so much as mourning it?

On the other hand, the Opata seem to have been complicit in their own oblivion. In the 1950s, the communities Roger Owen studied asked to remain anonymous.[6] This may be another example of a crypto, or hidden, culture much like the Jews in Mexico.

I do know that my great-grandmother, Pastora Curiel, considered herself an Opata. Pastora died young and left a fourteen-year-old daughter, who would marry shortly after her fifteenth birthday and become my grandmother. This is one of the few things passed on to her. I know that the Opata traveled to California and Chicago and many other places in pursuit of farm and railroad work. They worked as soldiers and scouts for the Spaniards, then the Mexicans, and then the Americans. Their history shows that they grew cotton and wove palm leaves and were brave fighters — including the women — and that the women held high status. At one point — along with the Yaqui and Mayo — the Opata fought against the Mexican government for the dream of an independent, indigenous state in northwestern Mexico.

I do know that on Palm Sunday I went to church at San Xavier del Bac, on the Tohono O'odham reservation south of Tucson, and wove palm into a cross along with hundreds of other people. I turned and looked back across the sanctuary, filled with pilgrims from the desert — light and dark, tall and short, most dressed in cotton dresses or wearing Stetsons, the older women with long, uncut hair to the floor — and realized that they were there — the Opata — mixed in with everyone else. They may no longer know who they are, or they may choose not to tell.

II

The word *holocaust* has been used, and perhaps overused, for many events over the years. Some disasters to which the term applies have been widespread and well documented, like the devastation of the Jews in Europe during World War II. Others have been regionalized, perhaps unnoticed or ignored by the outside world until it is too late. Even if a few die, it is too late for them. Even now, there are people whose lives are being shattered by others, who wonder, Will anyone care? What will tomorrow bring?

Over and over, history is filled with such manmade disasters. It is easy to go through the annals of a region and read about people being displaced or destroyed. Within twenty years, a new people might claim the same land as their ancestral homeland, because the previous occupants "left." One reason I wrote *The Flower in the Skull* was to try to particularize one of these histories. It happens to be my history, and one that I was not especially pleased to learn. I felt that by being as specific as possible, by portraying the experiences of one or two individuals, I might make it seem more real, less abstract. It is harder to bury such a history when names and places are attached. It is even harder when names and places are attached to people still living.

Until I researched this book, I did not realize that separating traditional people from their land is, in essence, a death sentence. When the landscape itself is holy, separation from it means the loss of one's holy places, the ceremonies and customs that honor those places, and often, the dissipation of the culture itself.

Elizabeth Cook-Lynn addresses this topic in her book *Why I Can't Read Wallace Stegner and Other Essays:* "The indigenous view of the world — that the very origins of a people are specifically tribal (nationalistic) and rooted in a specific geography (place), that mythology (soul) and geography (land) are inseparable, that even language is rooted in a specific place."[7]

In trying to understand why some people who are displaced survive and others perish, I spoke with historian Tom Sheridan, at the University of Arizona. I asked him why some cultures survive exile and persecution, like the Jews, and why some are scattered, like the Opata. He said that in traditional culture, place is sacred, so if a people are separated from the land, rituals are not fulfilled, crops are not planted, and the culture is destroyed. Without culture or land to hold them together, people scatter and are dispersed. This is why separating indigenous people from their land is so devastating, as demonstrated in the United States and Australia, as well as Mexico.

But when Moses came down off of the mountain with the stone tablets, the written word was made holy. And the word, unlike land, is portable. So the Jews were able to put the stone tablets in the Holy Ark and carry them off into exile, and with them, an intact culture and way of life. Considering the material I was working with in *Spirits of the Ordinary*, about the hidden Jews of Mexico, and *The Flower in the Skull*, about the Opata, this was a very valuable insight for me. I am greatly indebted to Dr. Sheridan for providing it.

But besides writing *The Flower in the Skull* in the spirit of "never forget," I wrote it because, as A. S. Byatt wrote, "We are all like Sheherazade, under sentence of death, and we all think of our lives as narratives, with beginnings, middles and ends."[8] We tell stories in order to stave off disaster. We delay the end while portraying the drama of human grace and folly. We delay the end to reproduce the mystery and inevitability of the shape of a human life. We delay the end in order to delay our own inevitable demise. We wait, and we search for the flower in the skull. In one account discovered by Byatt, Sheherazade gives birth to three children during the course of the 1,001 nights. The similarities to La Malinche, The Tongue and mother of our race, are hard to ignore.

After the publication of *The Flower in the Skull*, I received an e-mail from a woman in New York State. Her husband, she said, was Opata, and while they were very proud of this connection, they had no idea what it meant. So I sent them a list of sources for my book. This was the first direct contact I had with others from this background. Since then, I have heard from others, and now there are two Web sites and a chat group devoted to the Opata. I don't think this qualifies as a cultural revival, but it does mean that a corner of the veil has been lifted, and one more generation can see where we fit into the mosaic of human history. Context — including the landscape in which a people belong — is everything. I hope, someday, to publish an anthology of historical writing about the Opata, something that people can find in their libraries, and say, "Oh, yes, your grandfather was from Sonora, and those remind me of the stories he told."

As a writer, I probably treat the word as though it is holy, but I think what it represents, really, is the indestructible link between a people and their land. Words, like dragons' teeth, can be scattered on the empty landscape, watered with blood, and beget a new generation.

Your Grandmother Might Have Been Mayor
or Why Write?

When I was first asked to write this article, I declined, citing lack of time and the fact that there are "few Hispanic writers in the Northwest." As soon as I said that, I knew it wasn't true. There are few Hispanic/Latino writers being published in the Northwest, but I knew that people were at home writing.

So I will address this article to the writers of color who don't send out their work. Why write? Why submit your work for publication given all the odds against getting published?

First of all, people need to hear your voice. They may not like your voice, or even your grammar, but you are part of the cultural crazy quilt, too. Many editors say they receive few submissions from writers of color, and when they do, they are not of good quality. The editors who really want to publish your work will give thoughtful critiques and ask you to try again. These critiques might make you mad, so go ahead and throw that manuscript in a drawer and stomp around. When you've cooled off, look at the critique and see if there might be something useful in it. Rewrite the piece and send it out again. It takes time to get published, but eventually the right piece will find the right editor.

Practice, practice, practice. The more you write, the easier it gets. Write letters to the editor: It's an easy way to get published, and if you like seeing your work in print, a good incentive. Write to your relatives, even if they owe you money (or you them). Keep a journal, at least when you travel or have the opportunity to speak with elders. This leads to the next reason to write: history is usually written by the conquerors.

You probably went through school being told that your ancestors were ignorant slaves or migrant labor that came to this country at the bidding of rich, white industrialists; that they did your ancestors a big favor by inviting them to come and work for them. They rarely tell you what happened before that, or who owned the land before their ancestors showed up. Don't take other people's word for it. Do your own research. You might find that your great-grandfather was a respected healer, that your grandmother was mayor of the town where she grew up, and held off the Federalistas single-handedly with a shotgun and a broom. Or you might find that all of your father's family walked north to work on the railroad because there was such a need for labor in this country. Work is noble, too. Not only do these stories need to be told, they are a wonderful addition to the culture of any country. This heritage is yours to discover and share. By becoming a writer, you can *rewrite history*.

Finally, support other writers of color. Buy their books, take classes from them, seek them out to wish them well and ask for words of encouragement. The Northwest is blessed with some of the best writers in the country, such as Charles Johnson, Colleen Mc-Elroy, and Sherman Alexie. The more people of color are writing, the more editors and publishers have to take us seriously. Go to your local bookstore and ask for these books, even if you know the owner doesn't carry them. The next day, put on your sunglasses and ask again. Bookstore owners need to make money, and if they perceive a demand, they will carry more books by minority writers.

Finally, if you are in a position to do so, encourage others to write, and share the work of writers you like. Volunteer to go into classrooms — these are your future readers; read on the radio services for the blind — they need to hear your way of speaking and the type of literature that interests you. Read to the shut-ins and elderly, and they may share their stories with you.

Writing by people of color, no matter what your subject, is a political act — an important contribution to your community. So don't let people trivialize the time that you spend writing. Treat it as a devotion, as a religious act if need be. Even if it's just one half hour a day, it might be enough time to polish that story or finish that poem. And send out those manuscripts! Editors are standing by.

King County Arts Commission Newsletter, 1990

Pancho Villa Doesn't Sleep Here

.

I learned that I would be editing three issues of the Seattle Art Commission newsletter shortly before leaving on a long-planned trip to Mexico. I had proposed devoting one issue to artists who draw on their immigrant status or that of their forebears, either continuing a traditional art or exploring the themes of change and displacement. My own trip to Mexico was partly in search of material for a historical novel based on my great-grandparents.

It had been eighteen years since I set foot in Chihuahua, half my lifetime. Chihuahua was in the second year of a severe drought, and the air was searing. The two-hundred-mile drive from El Paso to Chihuahua revealed a landscape blasted by the sun. There was a new highway, however, with its virtues linked to that of the Chihuahua government in a series of signs, Burma Shave style.

Chihuahua is not a tourist destination. Over Labor Day weekend, we saw only four or five parties of Americans. Our hotel, chaotic by American standards, was inhabited mostly by Mexican businessmen in town to close financial deals at one of the many banks. Although a drought had devastated the area, leaving the city without running water most of the time, Chihuahua continued to thrive. Decaying Federalist-era buildings lean up against new construction, and Tarahumara Indians in bright skirts and headbands mingle with Sunday shoppers. Maquiladoras — huge, labor-intensive factories — have attracted people from all over Mexico to work here.

My cousins, childhood playmates, were grown women with families. One is married to a mining executive, one to a personnel trainer at a concrete company. We lapsed back into our former habit of their conversing in Spanish and my answering in a mixture of English and Spanish. This close to the border, everyone understands some English, and my husband even ventured a few words in Spanish.

One day we drove out to a town, Santa Isabel, we used to visit when I was a child, near a river with beautiful trees. I remembered that my aunt, wearing a loose cotton shift, used to wade into the water with a bar of soap and bathe. "It makes me feel really clean!" she used to say. On the way to the river, my cousin kept warning me that, because of the drought, everything had dried up. Instead, we found a beautiful oasis from the heat. For some political reason, Santa Isabel had been fixed up, and had the peaceful austerity of old New Mexican towns. The main square is full of trees and an intricately wrought iron bandstand, or zocalo, with light bulbs dangling from dragons' mouths. We ate paletas, locally made Popsicles of fresh, tropical fruits, and then drove down to the river. Though reduced to a stream by the harsh weather, the Santa Isabel river is still beautiful. My cousin's sons caught *pichiquates*, or polliwogs, while cattle lounged in the shallows a few yards downstream, their vaqueros keeping an eye on them from the shade.

What did I seek by coming back here? Not so much a confirmation of memory as those nuggets of reality that evoke memory. Like Marcel Proust and his madeleines, I could bite into a frosty mango paleta and bring back the smell, the feel, the quality of the air of Northern Mexico on a hot day. It is this evocation of memory that I expect to serve me well as I write my novel.

While the novel is set in the 1870s and centered in Saltillo, a city farther east and south, the Mexican countryside is timeless, and the cities retain a mysterious essence, a personality, if you like, that I hoped to capture in my writing. My great-grandfather visited Chihuahua, on a long journey that he and my mother's father took together, I don't remember why or where. My great-grandfather told people he was taking my grandfather to seminary to become a priest in order to get free food and lodgings. My grandfather retaliated by becoming a Methodist minister.

In the late afternoons, we sat in my maternal aunt's darkened living room and drank iced sodas. She shared bits and pieces of memory and lore about her grandfather. Much of it is scandalous by the standards of my conservative Protestant family, and she kept saying, "But it's okay, you can write what you like about us." The line between fiction and reality can sometimes seem blurry, and the longer I spent in Chihuahua, the fuzzier it got to me.

My aunt and uncle now live in a new house that had been under construction for years. It was about two blocks from the house on Calle de la llave that I had loved and visited every summer. The new house, cavernous and unfinished, seems too large for the two of them, and the house next door, with my cousin, her husband, and two sons, seems too small.

My Uncle Francisco was now in a hospital bed in a small room near the kitchen, where my aunt could keep up with her constant cooking while keeping him near. Formerly the director of a prestigious private school, a painter, poet, singer, and a voracious reader, my uncle was now limited by a series of small strokes that robbed him of sight and mobility. About two weeks earlier, said my aunt, my Uncle Francisco lay in bed lecturing one of his classes, as erudite and self-possessed as ever. His randomly accessible memory had tapped into that long-ago lecture.

I spent two long afternoons upstairs in my uncle's library. Although it was well over 100 degrees in the airless room, the variety and rarity of his books kept me glued there as long as I could see straight. Hundreds of volumes of history, fiction, philosophy, and natural medicine stood side by side with biographies of great painters and composers. Volumes of poetry, Methodist hymnals, and theology were mixed in. Some of the poetry and fiction were by our relatives and ancestors in Saltillo — María Narro Valdés, who was also a painter, her husband, José García Rodríguez, and the well-known poet, Manuel Acuña. Many of the books were personally signed to "Professor Francisco Cepeda."

Downstairs, my husband played with our baby while my aunt drifted back and forth between them and my uncle. Every Monday afternoon, a childhood friend of hers comes over for lunch. An epileptic, she can tell instantaneously by your birth date what day of the week your birthday will fall each year. I am not sure if her ability to compute numbers is related to her epilepsy.

Poring over the dusty books in Spanish, in that vast room in that vast unfinished house, I felt like a character in story by Jorge Luis Borges. My stories have been criticized for having unsatisfactory endings. Characters are revealed, but they often don't take a conclusive action that sums up their existence in the way that American short stories are supposed to end.

But how can I write that way? The hotel we stayed in, grandly called El Palacio del Sol, was under construction the whole time.

"Disculpe las molestias," said a sign in the lobby, *"Ocasionadas por remodelación — deseamos brindarle un mejor servicio."* "Pardon the bother," I think this means, "We are trying to bring you better service." They seemed to be turning the lobby into a disco. Is there a clear connection between the sign and the disco? Birthdays and epilepsy? Character and action?

Pancho Villa built himself an elaborate mausoleum in Chihuahua, but was assassinated and buried farther south, in Parral. Worse, his corpse was later dug up and the head stolen. Some say it is now at Yale in the possession of the Skull and Bones club, a secret society to which George W. Bush once belonged.

We visited Pancho Villa's former home in Chihuahua. I had been there many years before when his widow, Luz Corral, tried to make a little money by showing it to the public. Now called El Museo de la Revolución, it has been restored to its former ostentation, with fin de siècle furnishings and silk scarves on the two pianos. Big enough to hold a small army, it probably did at times. In a courtyard stands the open car in which Pancho Villa was shot, the bullet holes clearly visible in the side. Inside, alongside murals depicting revolutionary heroes, is a death mask of Villa showing the fatal shot in his forehead. There are several castings of the death mask, more significant, I suppose, since the original is missing.

"Too bad," said several of my cousins, "that they couldn't have fixed up the house when Luz Corral was alive, renting out the back rooms to make a living." I assured them that Luz Corral, one of many Mrs. Villas, but always claiming that she was the real one, probably haunted the house after museum hours, sitting on the brocade couches and running invisible hands across the sun-weathered upholstery of the death carriage. Villa, meanwhile, if he still haunts the land looking for his head, probably spends each night in a different town, as he used to with a new bride, just to check on the progress of his many grand- and great-grandchildren.

Chihuahua is a remarkable city, a frontier town that has continued to nurture the seeds of revolution. Chihuahua seceded from the federation and printed its own money at one point during the 1800s. The post office is built over the dungeon where Father Hidalgo, one of the revolutionary heroes, was held before his execution. For 500 pesos, you can descend the cool stone steps and view his cell. Driving around with my cousins one day, I saw "Rusos afuera de Lituania" spray painted at a busy intersection. This was before the end of the USSR.

"Are there Lithuanians in Mexico?" I asked one of my cousins.

"No," she replied, "but Mexicans always have to have their say." They have often paid in blood for that say.

My stories don't end in the conventional mode because these stories have not yet ended. I can tell a story, describe a circle, but each is merely a gear in a larger, clocklike mechanism that moves to the rhythm of the stars. Time is etched upon the face of Mexico in a way that makes its inhabitants and descendants familiar, even intimate, with their mortality. My characters sometimes continue their adventures after death, much as Pancho Villa has continued his.

What I was looking for in Mexico, of course, was a piece of myself. Every writer conjures up her characters from the well of self. Somewhere in that well, my great-grandfather, a drunk and a gold prospector, as well as a very resourceful man, continues to spin futures for himself. Somewhere else in that well, his wife, my great-grandmother, says her rosary and consults a lawyer about protecting her money. I saw them in the weary women on the streets of Chihuahua, the bankers, the Tarahumara Indians, the ranchers hard as barbed wire who would melt at the sight of my child and say, "What a pretty baby." This is what I sought: the humanity that would make my characters more than just constructions, the bone and silk and sweat and perfume that would make them live in the reader's mind.

As a scholar, I found treasures in my uncle's library that would provide the authenticity that I sought for my story — descriptions of place and dress, quotations from nineteenth-century writers and scholars. I spent hours translating portions of these books and fine-tuning my characters with the information. But as a person, I found the heart of Mexico, my own heart, never changing, always changing, always ready for a cold paleta, a bench in the shade, and a good story.

October 12, 1990

Francisco's Library

24 de Mayo 1990
Chih, Chih, Mex.

Chih. Is much the same to me, though big and dirty and noisy. Priscila says they have built *maquinaderas* (industrial towns) so people have come from all over, from the south, to work in them. Impoverished looking settlements, raw cement bricks with no trees, are springing up everywhere. There is not enough water for them. The land is stricken. I don't remember it ever so dry.

My aunt and uncle have moved. It's only a block from Calle de la llave, a street name I loved. They live on Paso Leal, and Priscila next door.

It looks beautiful walking in — a spacious tiled passageway full of plants one story high (the plants). It leads past a living and dining room on the right, a patio, a stairway on the left.

At the back, the kitchen on the right, a room with my uncle, now bedridden, on the left. He lies in a hospital bed, blind, unable to talk, but he responded to my talk and touch, and loved touching Ben's soft skin. He is 84. The rest of the room holds a big bed with a colorful spread, cozy furniture. This is clearly where my aunt spends her time. The upstairs is unused, the patio full of weeds. The back of the house peters out to a vacant lot.

26 de Mayo

Francisco was born on a hacienda near Saltillo of working people. 84 means he was born in 1906. Socially, Mexico had changed little from the 1500s to 1910, so he was born into the old class system, poor. He had to work since he was a boy, so it was important to him to have a big house once he could afford it. My husband and I walked around upstairs — one huge room after another, many with their own baths. There is no water connected upstairs. There is a big studio/library which I will visit tomorrow. On a drawing board is a pastel study of an owl. He had been painting owls before he lost his eyesight. Ruth and Prissy each have one. Julieta says I can take any painting I want, but I don't want to take any off the wall, although I love them. Some of the still lifes of cut papayas and flowers, obloid squash and tiny plums, are so vivid and so much a part of my permanent childhood memory that when I see them, I almost don't see them.

The land is dry. El llano en llanas. People yearn for rain.
Jan Feb Mar Apr May Jun Jul Aug Sept Oct Nov Dec
      Dry   Wet
      Easter   Christmas

27 de Mayo

Francisco's Library — Books all dusty and mixed up. Books on Mex history, esp. Northern Mexico; famous artists' biographies, bios of famous musicians and composers (classical); books on homeopathic and natural medicine; books on Christianity; world encyclopedias; many Spanish dictionaries; profiles of historic Mexican figures; popular novels by Mex. Writers; books from Spain; translations of books by Am. Authors — Pearl S. Buck, Hemingway, Dostoyevsky, Steinbeck. "Yo, Robot," por Isaac Asimov; a Spanish/English dictionary printed in the late 1700s. Books by relatives, including Manuel Acuña and José García Rodríguez. Books about Sor Juana; Gabriela Mistral; important women in world history.

∴ ∴ ∴ ∴ ∴

Many of the books in F's library had titles like "Hidden Pages," or "Stolen Pages," or the "Hidden Mexico."

The tables upstairs have bookends — a small, ornate globe — a colorful painting of birds on *cuero*, popular for the last 20 years or so — beautiful pottery on the bookcases. Priceless. Candy and wrappers left by Priscila's children. Photos and portraits of F. all over. Many of the books are inscribed by the authors to Prof. Cepeda.

Julieta played some really old gospel records for Wayne while I was upstairs. It sounded like Perry Como sings hymns or something. Scratched and well-used. She also knows all about Julio Iglesias. Ruth had recently traveled to Las Cruces to hear him.

⁘ ⁘ ⁘ ⁘ ⁘

Books

Medicamentos Indígenes, por Gerónimo Pompa, 1972
Relatos misterio y realismo, por José García Rodríguez, 1947
Los Mexicanos Pintados Por Si Mismos, orig. 1855, reprinted 1946
Cuentos del México Antiguo, por Artemio de Valle Arizpe, 1953
Antología de Poetas y Escrituras Coahuilenses, 1926
Los judíos bajo la inquisición en hispanoamérica, por Boleslao Lewin, 1960
Libro de Chilam Balam de Chumayel
Manuel Acuña, por Francisco Castillo Najera, 1950
Obras, por Manuel Acuña (poesías, teatro, artículos y cartas), 1965
Poesías de Manuel Acuña, segunda edición, 1968
Obras completas de Concha Espina, 1944

I am not a journal keeper. At an early age, I learned that nothing I wrote down was private, and so I learned to keep my private thoughts in my head. This probably gave me a very good memory, for even now, I can recall exact scenes from my childhood going back to age two.

Nevertheless, I realized that this was a special trip, different from the rest, because I was coming to Mexico of my own volition, a grown woman, and needed to gather material for my novel. I needed something to hold in my hands in the far north, in the rainy winter of Seattle and be able to say, "No, I didn't imagine it. It really *is* like that in Mexico. People really *do* sing in the streets and advertise cooked food for sale and the sky is bluer and the mangos sweeter. People *do* live in the moment instead of waiting for something better to come along." I needed to see my own handwriting telling me that "this is what Mexico is really like. I did not just imagine it." Of course, that's impossible, since we reimagine everything our senses tell us just as soon as it enters our brains. But still, I thought I would try.

The novel I was working on, which came to be called *Spirits of the Ordinary*, takes place in the late 1800s in a city another 500 miles east of Chihuahua. It is where my aunt's and mother's ancestors were from, and is not much known or written about. It is also difficult to get to from Seattle, Washington, and it would have been impossible to visit both Chihuahua and Saltillo in one trip. I opted for my living relatives, especially since my uncle was not expected to live much longer. Even though my son was less than a year old, I felt it was important for them to meet Ben, and I suppose there was sort of a "baptism of dust" involved in bringing Ben to Mexico, the home of his ancestors.

On the other hand, life in Northern Mexico has not changed all that much. Chihuahua is known for its Federalist (mid-1800s) architecture and its revolutionary history, and while the city is not the same, I felt that a lot of the ambiance would be duplicated in both Saltillo and Chihuahua. Both cities are commercial centers, rather than tourist destinations. Both cities have existed for several hundred years, and both have been heavily influenced by their proximity to the United States. Most interesting to me is the mixing of cultures — indigenous, Spanish, and European — that has been going on all this time, and the particularly fierce and independent outlook this has fostered in its people.

My uncle Francisco Cepeda Cruz was both unusual and typical of the citizens of Northern Mexico. Born to peasants on a hacienda, he became, at the age of 21, director of a prestigious private school in Chihuahua, a post he held for fifty years. Upon his retirement, he received a medal from the president of Mexico for his outstanding service to education. A devout Protestant, he was generous with his friends and silent about his enemies. As a child, I had found him both formidable and wonderful.

My uncle's library had been a source of curiosity since my childhood. It probably helped to shape my bookish nature as an adult, and I was eager to spend time in it, since I knew that it had invaluable source materials for my own writing. At the same time, I was interested in the space of the library, the idea of the library. I had come to realize, walking around Chihuahua, that architectural space in

Mexico reflects the public and private lives of people. Plazas, fountains, and grand buildings are set aside for communal use. Houses present a forbidding façade to the street, and are turned inward, built around an open courtyard where the family can move freely, and the division between interior and exterior is loosely defined. Catholic homes often have private shrines inside, and the idea of a personal library seemed even more private and interior to me. Perhaps, in our Protestant subculture, a love of learning had replaced faith in the institution of the Catholic Church.

It had not exactly been off limits to us as children, but we were not supposed to bother Francisco if he was working in his combination library/studio. With five children plus their friends and cousins, this was probably a matter of survival. Still, it retained an air of the tantalizingly forbidden, which I was to use for a library in *Spirits of the Ordinary:*

Within the enclosure was a miniature garden almost gemlike in its perfection. Low boxwood hedges hugged the wall on two sides, filling the air with their pungent odor. A veranda, or portico flanked the other two sides along the house. Next to the portico grew blood red roses, almost funereal in their intensity of color.

Huge pots of fuchsias hung from the protruding vigas of the portico, catching the sun and contrasting sharply with the deep shade against the house.

At the center of the garden, a fountain as squat as the house itself gurgled softly; the cold spring water spilled over its thick, green-stained lips and ran obediently along channels in the flagstone paving to form a shining ribbon that laced the garden in severe Moorish symmetry before disappearing under the hedges. The fountain had run steadily since the house was built, the springs within the earth seemingly inexhaustible.

Zacarías walked along the wooden portico to a small door and knocked. This was his father's study, and only the old man had a key to this door. After a moment, the door swung slowly inward, leaving Zacarías straining to see into the gloom of the interior before stooping to enter the doorway. His father was already reseated behind his massive desk, as though he had willed the door to open of its own volition.

The small, sallow-skinned man sat regarding his second son with large unblinking eyes like some nocturnal creature.

Zacarías always felt awkward in this study, large and clumsy among the fragile books and stacks of tissue-thin papers that would crumble to dust in a good gust of wind.

Here lay his father's treasure. Here were his books, the books accumulated one at a time, sometimes a few pages at a time, smuggled in saddle bags surrounding preserved foods, or wrapping a trinket from overseas. It had taken thirteen generations to compile this library, thirteen generations since all things Jewish, all signs of learning and Hebraic study had been burned by the townspeople of Saltillo, since Zacarías's forebears had gained the lives of their wives and children by changing their names and agreeing to be rebaptized into the Holy Roman Catholic Church.

Zacarías stood in this dark, crowded room, hemmed in by precariously balanced stacks of books, half-empty inkwells, broken quills and glass vials of mysterious chemicals. He stood too tall, his shoulders hunched under the weight of thirteen generations, under the name he bore, pinned against the six-inch thick door at his back by his father's unblinking gaze. Zacarías had no love of books, of tradition, or of enclosed places. He had come to tell his father goodbye.

·:· ·:· ·:· ·:· ·:·

One thing I discovered was that it was difficult to find information on women in Mexico in the late 1800s. I could find where all the trains ran, all the battle lines, all the crops, and the names of all the mines, but information on domestic life was scarce. I was interested in more than just the facts, of course. I wanted to know about attitudes and, most of all, what a woman in that time and place might have thought about herself, dreamed and aspired to, if anything. One clue came from a book in Francisco's library, and I copied out the table of contents:

Breves Biografías Intimas de Mujeres Celebres Españolas, 1949
Cleopatra
Teodora
Juana de Arco 1412–1431
Santa Teresa de Jesus

María Estuardo
Catalina de Erauso (la Monja Alfére)
Cristina de Suecia
Madame de Maintenon
Madame de Stael
Carlota Corday
La Malibrán
Carlota Bronte
Concepción Avenal
Sara Bernhardt
Condesa de Pardo Bazan
Jane Addams
Isadora Duncan

The main female character in *Spirits of the Ordinary* is Estela, a merchant's daughter who marries for love, then discovers that her husband is a wastrel, intent on spending their resources on prospecting for gold in the desert. Often alone with her children, the subject of gossip, she turns to books for solace:

> A sudden flight of birds, or movement of wind made Estela stop and gaze out the window. She could not say why, but she felt a lightness she had not felt in many years.
>
> She should feel terrible, thought Estela. Left alone to cope with the household by herself; her surly father, the prying neighbors; an abandoned woman. Estela tried to feel sorry for herself, something she had done often enough before, but today she could not.
>
> The last flowers of the season were still blooming. Her daughters played in the courtyard, their embroidery in a careless heap on a table. Gabriel read in a corner of the patio, his feet up, sweet tea at hand. My little man, she thought.
>
> Zacarías was gone again, but this time she had done something about it. Perhaps that was the difference.
>
> Leaving the kitchen, Estela wiped her hands on her apron and pulled it off over her head. She walked into the parlor and opened its wide windows onto the sunny yard. Normally reserved for guests, it stood unused most of the time. Estela picked a book of verse out of a shelf, sat down in the most comfortable chair near the window, and decided to read until it got too dark.
>
> Somewhere, a cock crowed, a horse whinnied, a cry of elote,

elote, roasted corn, floated on the evening breeze. She smelled sewage for a moment, followed by orange blossoms.

"Oh wretched moment of my birth," said the first verse she read,

When I opened eyes that one day would gaze upon you,
That one day would see the hand that never would be mine
Eyes that would see you speak the name of another,
See your lips tremble on that name . . .

Normally, Estela would find her heart beating rapidly when she read such things, but today the words were full of air. A pleasant light came in from the west-facing window, bathing her in its golden glow. Soon it would be too cool to enjoy the evenings like this. A light wind lifted the leaves of the trees, the wind from the mountains that blew everything clean, that cleansed the air of the town from the eternal dust of the desert.

⁖∿ ⁖∿ ⁖∿ ⁖∿ ⁖∿

My grandfather, Miguel Narro, unlike me, kept journals from his mid-teens until his death in 1955. A minister who traveled and lived all over the Southwest, his journals also functioned as his sermon notes and business records, but on occasion he included long descriptions of people and places otherwise lost. They include some of his dreams and his notes from teaching himself how to read Hebrew. I now have these journals, and they seem to radiate a magic of their own when I open the brittle covers and see his careful handwriting. They are his legacy to me, the only living writer in the family.

There is an air about life in Mexico that keeps it from ever seeming quite of this world. Perhaps it is true in all of Latin America, where the past and present run together, where reality is defined as much by faith as by scientific evidence. No amount of journal-keeping can pin down this quicksilver quality, which is just as well. In any case, I came across a paragraph that seemed to sum this up, and I hope that it applies not only to the books in Francisco's library, but to my writing as well:

Foreword to "La Mandrágora," a story in the *Anthología de la Literatura Fantástica Española*, 1969, edited by Jose Luis Guarner:

La presente historia, aunque verídica, no puede leerse a la claridad del sol. Te lo advierto, lector, no vayas allanarte a engaño: enciende una luz, pero no eléctrica, ni de gas corriente, ni siquiera de petróleo, sino uno de esos simpáticos velones típicos, de tan graciosa traza, que apenas alumbran, dejando en sombra la mayor parte del aposento. O, mejor aún, no enciendas nada; salta al jardín, y cerca del estanque, donde las magnolias derraman efluvios embriagadores y la luna rieles argentinos, oye el cuento de la mandrágora y del barón de Helynagy.

This story, although truthful, cannot be read in the clear light of the sun. I advise you, reader, don't try to deceive yourself: turn on a light, but not electric, not of gas, nor of petrol; perhaps one of those quaint lanterns, so graceful-looking, that barely cast any light, leaving in shadow a major part of the room. Or better yet, don't light anything; go outside to the garden, and near the pond, where the magnolias pour out their intoxicating fumes and the moon makes silver tracks, hear the story of the mandrake and the Baron of Helynagy.

The Writer's Journal, 1997[1]

A True Story

This is a true story, but I have never told it before. It might be a ghost story. It might even be the witnessing of a miraculous apparition, as told by an unbeliever. All I can tell you is what happened.

When I was seven, my parents bought a house in San Bernardino, California. Prior to that time, we had lived in Devore Heights, a mountain community where my father had been superintendent of a home for delinquent boys.

When he lost that job, my father worked as a substitute teacher in the San Bernardino schools, and we rented a house for a year. I loved that house, in a real neighborhood full of children, with a crepe myrtle tree in front where I spent many hours — daydreaming, reading, or spying on the neighborhood. But my mother was anxious to own a house, and when this one became available, we went to look at it.

The house was on the corner of 16th and H streets, a busy intersection two blocks from the high school. It was a good location for my family, with two sisters in high school, and not too far from where my father eventually landed a permanent job — Franklin Junior High. More important, while it was a mixed-race neighborhood, the house had been owned by a Mexican American couple. This is important, because San Bernardino realtors engaged in blatant redlining — the practice of confining people by race to certain neighborhoods. Because the house was already owned by Mexicans, they could sell to us.

I, of course, did not understand these things at the time. What I noticed when we went to see the house was a grown-up couple who were no taller than I was — both under five feet tall. There was a steady yapping coming from the bathroom, and eventually the wife brought out a trembling Chihuahua dog that fit into her cupped hands. I had never seen anything like it.

There were two odd things about the house. One was that, while the downstairs was built to standard dimensions, the upstairs was scaled for the diminutive couple who had built it. The slanted ceilings rose to a maximum height of six feet, and the bathroom sink and counters were low. Worse, the shower hit most people in about the middle of the chest.

The other odd thing was a huge liquor cabinet that dominated the dining room. Across the top of it was carved, "Pick Your Poison," and it was filled with mugs in the shape of human skulls. I couldn't take my eyes off of it. It looked like something in which a witch would keep her brews and potions. I finally asked what it was. The woman laughed and said it was sort of a joke and that a friend had made it for them. My mother said, "But it won't stay with the house, will it?" and the woman said no. My mother looked very relieved. She thought drinking alcohol was really evil, and probably thought the couple was practicing witchcraft, as well.

My parents decided to buy the house for twelve thousand dollars, a good price even in 1962. We thought it was very grand to live in a two-story house, something of a novelty in Southern California.

But that first night, I woke to strange noises. It sounded as though someone was moving heavy furniture across the ceiling of the bedroom I shared with one of my sisters. It was very noisy, but my sister slept through it. When I complained in the morning, I was told that it was just the house settling, that I would soon get used to the unfamiliar surroundings.

It happened the next night, and the next. I woke my sister during the height of it one night, and she sat up and listened as a chair seemed to be pulled across the ceiling, followed by footsteps. We raced downstairs and got my father out of bed. He got a flashlight and peered into the attic crawlspace, hardly more than two feet high.

"There's nothing there," he said, not happy at being rousted out of bed. "Maybe animals."

So I was discouraged from sharing my fears as the invisible upstairs neighbors constantly moved their belongings around, and walked back and forth across the thin ceiling. There were never voices or other sounds of life, but there were other strange occurrences.

At dusk, odd green lights would appear at the top of the stairs. They looked like reflections through glass, perhaps reflected off the knickknacks my mother had in open shelves along the stairway above the living room. Once, curious, I carefully closed all of the doors that opened onto the landing. But as I narrowed the last door through which I was peering, standing in my bedroom, the lights did not diminish one bit, and I flung open all the doors and turned on the lights as a chill swept over me — there was no discernible source for the lights.

Everyone had a theory about the sounds. It was the wood in the house contracting each night, since the temperature differences between night and day were so great. It was the house getting old. It was mice. It was rats. It was raccoons. It was my imagination.

But I was not the only one to hear the noises. Even during the day, when we were downstairs, we often heard someone approach the landing from upstairs and begin to descend. When my mother's piano students in the living room turned their heads to see who it was, there was no one there. The cat even heard the steps.

Mostly, I was left to cope with the noises by myself, since my oldest sister soon left for college, and my other sister was a heavy sleeper. After a couple of years, she, too, was gone most of the time, and I was left alone in the sweltering upstairs bedroom. The noises had diminished in sound level and frequency over the years, but I had become a habitual insomniac by then, listening to the sounds of the night — the cars, the trains, the lone walker returning home down empty streets. My uncle had given me an inexpensive walkie-talkie set one Christmas, and I discovered that I could pick up the police band on it. I could listen to the calls and track the sirens as they crisscrossed the sleeping city, knowing there were other people out there awake and getting into trouble.

∴ ∴ ∴ ∴ ∴

One night when I was about ten, the noises came back with their former intensity. I was really scared. They seemed more menacing this time, more purposeful. I looked out to the hallway and could see the green lights there, strong and angular. They seemed to be advancing towards me, growing stronger. I shut my eyes and I prayed, I asked God to protect me from whatever it was that stayed in that house. And something extraordinary happened. I opened my eyes, and a blue form began to take shape near the ceiling. It seemed to be the curved shape of a woman, sort of floating on her side, and with the image came an extraordinary sense of calm.

I could tell that she had come at my request, or at least allowed me to see her, for it seemed that she had been there all along. She was blue and glowing and beautiful, and seemed to be encased in an aura of light that radiated out from her. She hovered in the air near my bed, but between me and the green lights. And within moments, I relaxed and went to sleep. After that, the lights and noises came back now and then, but they never really bothered me, as I knew that the blue image was there, somewhere, to keep things from getting out of hand.

At the time, the child of practical Mexican Protestants, I had almost no imagery with which to describe this apparition. I thought she must be my guardian angel, and was reassured to find that I had one. She also seemed to me somewhat fairylike, since one of my aunts had brought me picture books about the wee folk from England. But everyone knows there are no fairies in Southern California, at least not that kind.

∴ ∴ ∴ ∴ ∴

Only many years later did I see any images that reminded me of the woman in blue light. It was when Seattle artist Alfredo Arreguín showed me some paintings he had done of the Virgin Mary. By then, of course, I had seen many representations of her, and the Virgin of Guadalupe in particular. Alfredo had also painted many different aspects of the Virgin Mary over the years, usually an indigenous Mary surrounded by flowers and vines, like the one on the cover of my first book. But these new paintings had not only the same shape as the image I had seen, almost an organic paisley shape, but also the same quality of light. It seemed to radiate out from the canvas and enfold the viewer in a compassionate embrace.

Alfredo said that he had recently donated one of these images to a Latino senior center constructed by El Centro de La Raza. When the painting was unveiled, he said, much to his astonishment, people fell to their knees and crossed themselves. They venerated the image of La Virgen he had given them. I could see why. The jewel-like tones of his painting, the overall shape and attitude of the figure seemed to embody the nonjudgmental love that we all seek, and many attribute to the Virgin.

So was my childhood experience a miracle? It was to me, so I suppose that's all that matters. Had I been a Catholic child, perhaps I would have vowed to become a nun right then and there. Fortunately, I wasn't. But it is an image that I will always treasure, and on which I know I can always call when the noises of the world seem ready to overwhelm me.

❖ III ❖
A Star of David

The Skeleton in the Closet

She first suspected that something had changed when the yellow roses began to bloom in the weeds at the edge of her porch.

∴ ∴ ∴ ∴ ∴

This is the first sentence of a story I wrote for my creative writing workshop with Joanna Russ at the University of Washington. It was late at night when I began, and I was restless. My husband and I had moved to Seattle the previous September, and we were renting a tiny house with not much room for pacing. I began as a graduate student winter quarter, and I was terrified that this was something I would not be able to do — write without impediment, allow the words to flow before the censor built into my head clamped down.

Amalia had never noticed the rosebush before, but she was delighted with it. Yellow was her favorite color. She began to water and coddle the roses, humming an old hymn as she worked.

"Here, Jana. You want a pretty flower?" she said to the little neighbor girl. Jana wouldn't look at the rose, only at Amalia's outstretched hand.

As part of my restlessness, I even cut bangs into my hair. Something was building inside of me, I just wasn't sure what, until I wrote that first sentence. Then, as though a pressure valve had been released, I was able to get into bed and sleep.

When the girl turned and ran into her house, frightened, Amalia realized that only she could see the yellow roses.

One of the reasons that writing this story was so difficult was that it was based on my own family. I grew up surrounded by stories, but in that time and place, stories were told for a specific reason. Not to entertain, but for didactic reasons — to provide moral guidance and example. To tell a story just to tell a story, for pure entertainment, felt like a form of heresy. But it was a form to which I was irresistibly drawn.

When I began taking family stories and recasting them in the fictional form, I was not sure how my family would feel. My mother was from a large, insular family, and most of the stories I knew came from her brothers and sisters. The stories concerned the many places they had lived growing up as the children of a Mexican Protestant minister and his wife, our ancestors, eccentric personalities, and the unexplainable. At the same time, these stories were mostly not told outside of the family. Somehow, they would mark our otherness to people, or be too complicated to explain outside of the context of known family history — you had to be brought up in these stories to understand them.

When I began writing my stories, I showed a couple of them to my mother. Her comments were things like, "He didn't die of typhoid, he died of scarlet fever." Or, "We don't really know what happened after that," or, "Who's going to read this?"

These family stories, whether commonplace or fantastical, were told as history. The meaning of the story was based not on its factuality, but its intent. Once their point was made, the stories were often incomplete. Whatever happened to the maid carrying the knife? I would wonder. Where did our great-grandfather end up after our great-grandmother kicked him out of the house? How did she feel about it? No one in my mother's generation seemed to care. But like Paul Harvey, the old radio commentator, I wanted to hear the rest of the story.

I began writing fiction in order to explain the world to myself — there were too many fragmented or unfinished stories around me. This might be typical of my generation, the children of immigrants. When people leave the place where their families have lived for generations, the geographical context — the mountains, the village — is left behind. Names are changed when people cross borders, second languages do not hold the same meanings as the first.

My stories seemed to make my mother nervous. What was it that she was so worried about? Were there deep secrets to be uncovered? Scandal? Had someone in our family actually had sex? Difficult to believe.

Most of the stories were from the era just prior to the Mexican

Revolution, and it was a time about which I knew very little. For Mexicans living in the United States, Mexican history seems to begin with the Revolution of 1910, when most of my parents' generation came north. The identity of Mexican American was born in these revolutionary fires, as that of Chicano was forged in the 1960s in the fires of East L.A. My father was a refugee from Central Mexico who walked north with his family as a child. His parents went to work for the Santa Fe Railroad, living in Kansas and Illinois before settling in California. My mother's family lived for two or three years at a time in cities all over Northern Mexico and the United States. When the Revolution heated up, my grandfather managed to get appointed to churches on this side of the border.

From books, I learned how people lived in the days before the Revolution. I learned about civil law and the Constitution of Mexico after independence from Spain. I looked for books on how people dressed and ate, where the railroads ran.

When a friend sent an invitation to his wedding in Los Angeles, I called an aunt in Monterey Park whose garage was the unofficial family archive.

"I'm going to be in Los Angeles for a friend's wedding next month," I said, "and I wondered if I could come over and look through the papers in your garage for some writing I'm doing."

"That's fine," she said. "I'll use that as an excuse to clean it out. It's time. Just be sure and call before you come over."

When I got there in my rented car, the third load of old papers was on its way to the dump. Arcelia had hired someone with a station wagon to help her, and he had gotten to work well before I arrived. Nevertheless, I recovered most of my grandfather's journals from around 1900 to the 1950s. They contained lists of people and the places he had worked for all those years. They contained ticket stubs and light bills, missionary pamphlets, financial accountings, and inspirational sayings to include in his sermons, such as this snippet from an article called "Manly Greatness," by the Reverend H. L. Powers: "All of the persuasive power of the king's officers to get Daniel to do wrong was but to fail. His manly principle was greater than all of the Babylonian empire, and the king besides." Occasionally, there were detailed descriptions of places, and even more rarely, accounts of how my grandfather felt or what he thought of something. The journals were artifacts of time and place.

Within half an hour, my mother was also there. She had insisted that my father drive her out from San Bernardino, since she never drove on the freeway. She stood beside me as I picked through the mouse-eaten papers. Each time I picked up something, she would say, "What do you want *that* for?" or "What are you going to do with it?" Her unease was palpable, contagious. Faced with her constant obstructions, I found my will to go through this overwhelming amount of material in two or three hours beginning to slip.

I finally sat her down in a lawn chair with a pen and a photo album and asked her to write the name of each person she recognized in it. In some cases, the only place to write was on the front of the photos, which ruined them, but it bought me the time I needed to fish the rest of my grandfather's journals out of the knee-deep pile of papers that still covered the garage floor. Most of the journals were in the sort of cheap composition books once required of schoolchildren, and after awhile, I began to be able to spot them. As my "keep" pile grew, I emptied a metal suitcase and filled it with my loot.

My mother had always been reticent about the family stories, but her sisters, especially Julieta, were not. I could count on our visits to Chihuahua every summer while I was growing up as a chance to learn a little more about our family. When three of the sisters were together — Julieta, Lydia, and Rosa Fe — they seemed to stimulate the urge in each other to tell stories.

My uncles were more taciturn, but also knew different versions, or different stories. For many years, Thanksgiving was celebrated at my Aunt Arcelia and Uncle Pablo's house. We celebrated it not as a national holiday, but as a religious one, a time to give thanks for the bounty of God's grace. The pilgrims, wherever it was they landed, were incidental to our understanding of the holiday. The ranch-style house in Monterey Park saw us at many stages of our growing up, from little children to adults with children of our own.

We arrived at the house sometime between noon and two, after an hour's drive from San Bernardino. This made four families, and sometimes a guest came along or was invited directly by my aunt and uncle. The house filled with the shrieking of little girls in fancy dresses and one boy cousin, Pablito, running around, until Pablito decided he was too old for that and tried to preserve his dignity.

Because the house was not large, we strung a series of tables together starting at the kitchen, extending the length of the dining room, and making an L into the living room. The last part of the L was a smaller table at which the children sat, far from the action of the kitchen and out from under Arcelia's feet. In that way, maybe twenty people could be accommodated. As we grew older, we were allowed to sit somewhere else along the table.

My aunt by marriage, Arcelia prepared almost all of the food, although other families brought token salads or desserts. She always prepared a turkey or two, along with other traditional Mexican foods such as refried beans, Spanish rice, squash, baked yams, and sometimes tamales, although they were usually reserved for Christmas. As they got older, her two daughters began to help, and one of them prepared a wonderful salad with lemon and tiny shrimp in it. I thought it was the best thing I had ever tasted, and have loved shrimp ever since.

After a lengthy prayer that more closely resembled a sermon, delivered by my father or one of my uncles, we ate until we were sated, then thanked my aunt for all her work.

"There are other things I would like to try and cook," she said, "like a goose. I'd like to try and stuff a goose sometime. Or lamb. But I know your Uncle Eduardo would not eat it, and I need to prepare food for everyone."

Then my Uncle Miguel leaned across the table and said to me, "You know the story about Eduardo, don't you?"

"Something about a pet lamb," I answered, although I knew perfectly well what the story was about.

"It wasn't meant to be a pet," my Uncle Pablo would say. "We were a big family, and our father didn't earn very much money, so people would give us things sometimes, clothing, or food. Once someone, I don't remember who . . ." a discussion about who it might have been followed at this point, ". . . gave us a lamb."

"But instead of preparing it right away, we kept it for a while," Uncle Miguel chimed in. "And it got attached to your uncle, and began to follow him around."

By this time, Uncle Eduardo had stopped eating and pushed his plate away from himself a little bit.

"But of course we were very poor," said Uncle Pablo, "and we could not afford to feed an animal just to keep it."

Here there was an awkward pause. "My mother did the best she could," Uncle Eduardo said. "And I was hungry, but when she served that lamb, I just could not eat it."

"But we did," Uncle Miguel would say. "I guess it wasn't very nice of us."

At this point, Uncle Eduardo stared sorrowfully into his plate, as though he could still see those slices of meat there. "And I still won't eat lamb," he said. "I guess in memory of that lamb. That's my protest."

It was the same every year. I don't know if Arcelia felt that she had to start the story, and I don't know if it hurt Eduardo every year to have it told. But this was a family that seemed to need guilt and internal pain, as though this mortification, this lashing of the soul, was a necessary part of the Thanksgiving ritual.

The day came to a close when someone handed a guitar to my mother, or when she opened the lid on the little spinet piano, and the adults began to sing the songs of Agustín Lara, those old, nostalgic songs about love and Mexico and loneliness — "Solamente una vez," "Janitzio." It would end with the adults in tears. Although the family was very bad at expressing feelings for each other, singing seemed to provide the emotional release they needed to complete a family gathering. By now the children were hot and grumpy and tired, ready to go home or have the rest of us leave the house. As the sun was going down, back into the station wagon we went, and back to San Bernardino for the long weekend without school or work.

My Uncle Eduardo never married. He worked for Hughes Aircraft for many years, and still lives in an apartment not too far from the former headquarters in Long Beach. When we were little, he didn't talk to the children much. But now that we are grown, and most of his brothers and sisters are gone, he seems to like us more. He is interested in old movie stars and old books, solitary activities. He was his mother's youngest, and when he wanted to nurse as a child, he would take her a book. So books are still his comfort and companions.

⋰ ⋰ ⋰ ⋰ ⋰

In many cases, after the point of a story was made, it would dissolve or branch into a related story. For example, a story was told of visiting a church in Mexico where people shared a common communion cup. One of our cousins told my sister that people spit the "wine" back into the cup, so she refused to drink when it was passed to her. I'm sure my cousin was not telling the truth, but conversation then turned to other stories about the odd practices of this church, rather than following up on the consequences of refusing the communion cup, which is how a fictional story would be told — focusing on the inner life of one character.

These tangential stories served to provide a context for the primary stories. They were part of the web of family and culture that gave meaning to the stories, and also made them so difficult to tell in isolation to someone from another family or culture, which was just about everyone. I recognized this web of stories when I read *Yellow Woman and the Beauty of the Spirit*,[1] by Leslie Marmon Silko. Individual stories can be told, but there is always the assumption of a larger body of stories within which the single story is understood.

So what was my mother so afraid of? What could be more wholesome than a family full of preacher's kids? The story about Amalia poured out of me over the next few days, and even after editing, remained virtually unchanged from the first draft. Amalia, although not her real name, was about someone I knew. It was about one of my mother's other sisters, who was still very much alive at the time.

Every family has stories of eccentricity, of madness, of feeble-minded members, alcoholism, addiction, lust, abandonment, illegitimacy. Our family was no exception. But were there any real skeletons in the closet? Earthshaking secrets that would cause people to cross the street to avoid us?

There were skeletons, but not sexual — although some of that — and not financial, but something else altogether.

．ヾ ．ヾ ．ヾ ．ヾ ．ヾ

The skeletons in our closet turned out to be ethnic and religious. When my aunts and uncles described my grandfather's conversion, they would say, "No se pegó el catolicismo" — the Catholicism did not stick. That's because, I eventually realized, it was pasted on over a Jewish soul.

One of the family stories was that we were descended from two brothers who came from northern Spain in the late 1700s. They were Jewish. I didn't think too much of this when I was young, and figured we were merely an anomaly among our Mexican American neighbors, who were all good Catholics, with a couple of Baptist families thrown in. We were, as far as I knew, the only Mexican Jewish Protestants on the planet. I began researching this aspect of our family only as part of the whole fabric of life in nineteenth-century Mexico. Through the historical writings of Vito Alessio Robles[2] about Northern Mexico, I learned that Saltillo, the city where my ancestors settled, had been the site of a terrible chapter of the Spanish Inquisition. The governor of the province, Luís Carva-jál, was accused, along with several members of his family, of being a practicing Jew. He died in prison, and five of his relatives were ex-ecuted by the auto-da-fé. This happened before the arrival of my ancestors, but showed that they came to the New World to join an existing community of Jews. This was the first association I had made between my family and the Inquisition. As a relative said re-cently, "That explains a lot."

Jews who came to Mexico before its independence from Spain in 1840 were almost always Conversos — people who had converted to Catholicism, or Marranos — an archaic, derogatory term for se-cret Jews. Those who continued to practice their religion did so discreetly even into the twentieth century. So discreetly, in some cases, that they had little idea what the rituals in their lives actually meant. The symbols remained, but the body of knowledge and re-ligious learning behind them had slowly been lost over the years.

The family stories I grew up with had this background of hidden Judaism as a larger context. The reticence to share family history with others, the dislike of Catholicism and Catholic symbols, even the network of odd Protestant congregations, were all part of this legacy. The melancholy veil of secrecy that shrouded family gather-ings, and the accompanying stories, were due to the habit of survival.

Though most of the stories would not raise an eyebrow in the polyglot, multiethnic and religious United States of the twenty-first century, five hundred years of conditioning had created a clan of very cautious people. Becoming the subject of racism directed at all Mexicans in the United States did nothing to relieve this attitude of circumspection. The need to keep your head down, blend in, and do your job dovetailed with the earlier strategies for survival that had kept my ancestors alive all these years.

Since the late 1980s, when I began this research on my own,

crypto-Judaism has been more openly discussed, and even become the subject of academic inquiry. A few useful books have been published, and a nonprofit group, the Society for Crypto-Judaic Studies, meets regularly to present papers and share resources.

The story of my maternal grandmother was another told only incompletely. There were no Irish last names in the family, but this mystery was never explained to me when I was little. These family stories — the Catholicism not sticking, the Irish ancestor — were only told only in part in an attempt to preserve family history without putting us in danger, or impugning the honor of individuals. My mother's family was acutely aware of what was considered proper, acceptable behavior, and each of them, at one time or another, had been curbed or chastised for straying too close to its boundaries. Perhaps because they had so little material wealth, reputation came to take on a greater value than it would have if the family had stayed Catholic, stayed in Saltillo, and remained part of the social system my grandfather deliberately cast aside.

In my hunger for stories, I discovered a group of people who typified the Southwest. When the history of the area is looked at in a broad sense, it is the result of many in-migrations, even before the arrival of the Europeans. It has always been a place of trade and cultural mixing, of liaisons both licit and illicit, and of refuge for oppressed peoples fleeing other areas — from my great-grandmother's people, an offshoot of the Puebloans pushed south into the Sonoran Desert, to my Jewish ancestors, and even my Irish great-grandfather, who worked in a mine in Arizona. Day by day, year by year, individual by individual, these people had lived out the consequences of war, of economic flux, of cultural and religious oppression, of poverty, of hope, of endurance. The one thing they had in common was the ability to begin again.

When I finished doing all the research, I understood my own connections to history and geography. More than just an intellectual exercise, or even an emotional or spiritual journey, this writing and research tied me to history as a whole.

‧ⱴ ‧ⱴ ‧ⱴ ‧ⱴ ‧ⱴ

Writing about family history has taught me that much of who we think we are is based on the unexplainable. And, in writing, I must follow those impulses and urgings in order to make a coherent whole. Often a hunch or an impulse leads to the information or material that can form the basis of a story, or even a book.

A few days after I began the story of Amalia, I received a note from my mother that the character I called Rosetta in the story, Amalia's sister, had died a few days before I got the letter. She died, it turned out, the night I began writing that story, probably moments before I put the first sentence on paper. To this day, I do not know what prompted me to write the story that night.

This is how the story ends: *And so, not knowing how else to tell it, I have written this story. The Indians in this part of the country, the Northwest, have a term,* sheel-shole, *which means "to thread the bead." It refers to a way of traveling from inland to the ocean by guiding a boat from one interconnected lake to the next. My aunt Amalia is still alive, but it's only a matter of time before she paddles her canoe, yellow roses and all, out into the open sea.*

The real "Amalia" lived for many years after. She read my story, along with my other books and stories, and liked them very much. She was proud of the fact that I became a writer, and paraded me around the nursing home where she lived. By the end, she was agoraphobic, and refused to go outside for any reason. Later, afraid of falling, she confined herself to a wheelchair. Her world, always small, always interior, got smaller and smaller. She never owned much, living at the mercy of her relatives and public assistance, never with a thought that she was "owed" anything more. She died a week before I wrote this essay.

There are more stories about Amalia, some sad, some happy. I'm not sure yet how to tell them, if at all. The skeletons I found in the closet were not frightening or scandalous. They were ghosts, moths, fireflies. I found faded photographs, good intentions, and the glowing embers of a sort of fatalistic optimism.

What I do know is that a writer's main job is to always be open to the possibilities of story. Like the interconnected lakes, old stories lead to new ones, and lead to new ways of seeing and living in the world. Like Amalia clutching her yellow roses, I will continue to follow these stories wherever they lead me.

September 24, 2003

A Star of David on Christmas

I

It is Christmas Day, and my relatives are visiting me on Bainbridge Island. They are spending the holiday here because my father recently moved from California to a retirement center nearby.

My oldest sister, I will call her Victoria, is wearing a Star of David against her red Christmas sweater. At first I am not going to say anything, but I know she is dying for someone to notice, so I decide to get it over with.

"It belonged to our mother," she says. "I think Julieta gave it to her."

My Aunt Julieta lives in a Jewish retirement center in El Paso, Texas. She wears a Star of David, as does her oldest daughter, in Chihuahua.

I decide to show Victoria copies of a newsletter I had received a few days earlier. It is called *Halapid*, the newsletter of the Society for Crypto-Judaic Studies.

"These are wonderful," she says. "Can I have them?"

"They just arrived, and I haven't read them yet. But I can make you copies."

Victoria is, as far as I know, a Baptist. Her daughter, whom I will call Heidi, lives in Spain, where she is a Protestant missionary. When I tell this to people, they say, "I didn't know they needed missionaries in Spain."

There were always stories in our family of Jewish ancestry, stories that I dismissed as a yearning for anything exotic, until I did some research myself. It turned out that there was a substantial community of crypto-Jews in Monterrey and Saltillo, Mexico, a community that our family joined relatively late in history, the 1790s.

I looked in my grandfather's journals for evidence of his feelings towards his Jewish ancestry, but all I found were a few pages on which he wrote out the Hebrew alphabet and a brief pronunciation guide, as though he were taking lessons from someone.

By the time I was in high school, we faced race riots daily between blacks and whites. This was when SWAT teams were first formed all over Southern California based on the example set by the LAPD under Police Commissioner Darryl Gates. Police in full combat gear descended on the high school and filled the corridors with tear gas until we were all subdued. Then we were called out by race to get on busses and go home.

The Jews were definitely white, and got bussed home with the white kids. I, on the other hand, lived in a neighborhood that was mixed, and, at least once, no bus driver would enter my neighborhood after one of the riots. It was a long walk home. At least as a Mexican, I got to remain neutral during the riots—I didn't have to fight either the blacks or the whites. From the safety of the art room, I remember watching two Chicano gang members standing on a planter one tear-gas-filled morning, watching the waves of students battle it out all around them. But the social order was rigid—each race to its own territory, no crossing over, no in between. Interracial dating was discussed, but not practiced. When the high school quarterback's prominent black family bought a house in an upscale section of town, the neighboring houses bloomed with For Sale signs almost immediately. College offered me the opportunity to leave San Bernardino, get a degree and some work experience, and eventually I returned to school to study writing. In 1990 I traveled to Chihuahua with my husband and new son to visit my relatives and use my uncle's library. That was the first time I saw my Aunt Julieta wearing a Star of David. I tried to get more stories out of her, or at least some details, but all she could remember were the same truncated stories of the two brothers from Spain, maybe two rabbis. I could not even figure out why, at this particular time in her life, she had begun to wear a Star of David. In that house full of books and mementos, she could offer me no concrete proof of anything, not even our own existence. In classic tales, things occur in threes, but our family stories gravitated to the incomplete number two, always lacking a resolution.

❖ ❖ ❖ ❖ ❖

On December 27th I took my sisters and their families to the nearby town of Poulsbo. My house, with nine people in it, had been getting smaller and smaller every day. Poulsbo is a Scandinavian tourist town with bakeries and antique stores.

We were in one of the stores when Victoria came over carrying a large, heavy menorah.

"This looks really old," she said. "Do you think it's old?"

"I don't know," I said. "Why don't you ask the owner?"

"Is this really old?" asked my sister.

"It's made to look old," said the proprietor, who was nearby. "If it were really old, it would cost much more."

It seemed expensive to me for a reproduction, and she would have to take it home on the plane. Remembering what the Sephardic scholar, Isaac Maimon, had told me, I said,

"You can probably buy a menorah in Spain, since people are openly admitting that they are Jewish." She planned to join her daughter there.

"If your heart says to buy it, then follow your heart," said my husband, surprising me. Normally, he stays out of these things.

"Oh," she said. "You think I should?"

"No," I said. "But you have to decide for yourself."

So she bought it.

∴ ∴ ∴ ∴ ∴

A day or two later Victoria returned to California and began preparations for her trip to Pamplona, not far from the supposed home of our ancestors on the French side of the border, Nyer. On her previous visit to Spain, she called up Narros in the phone book and asked if they were Jewish. They said no.

When I found "Narro," our mother's family name, in the phone books for San Antonio, Tucson, Mexico City, and Albuquerque, I refrained from calling them. I also refrain from calling the "Curiels" in the phone book when I am in Tucson and asking them if they are Opata Indians, like my great-grandmother, though I really want to know. These are things that people keep to themselves for reasons of social status and, in the past, kept to themselves in order to keep their lives. Recently, I have tried to become more open about my heritage, in part to hear stories from others.

In Mexico City in 1998, I tried to explain my background to a prominent Catholic family after the mother asked my religious persuasion. One of the sons published a literary magazine and was a friend of a friend. They had invited me to lunch at their home.

"Oh, yes," said another of the sons, a journalist. "I know some Narros. They're Jewish."

⋰⋱ ⋰⋱ ⋰⋱ ⋰⋱ ⋰⋱

After my sisters left, my husband and I speculated on Victoria's future. Always the good daughter, she married the person picked out by my parents and endured ten years of a miserable marriage before divorce. Perhaps, we say, she will move to Spain, convert, and marry a nice Jewish businessman. Someone who could take care of her, which is all anyone, including Victoria, ever wanted.

Victoria was always a straight-A student and worked as an elementary school teacher, but she lacked common sense. Once, many years before, she sent me a postcard of a fossilized dinosaur footprint. In it is visible a human footprint. "This is proof" she wrote, "that humans and dinosaurs existed at the same time!"

Before she left our house on that Christmas visit, I shared one more fact with Victoria that I picked up while in Mexico City. In 1791, the Jews of France were granted full citizenship rights. It was a window that closed again by 1815, but the date coincides with that of the two Narro brothers coming to Mexico to seek their fortune. It might have meant their papers did not say they were Jews, as had been the case before, and might have made their immigration possible, or at least, easier.

⋰⋱ ⋰⋱ ⋰⋱ ⋰⋱ ⋰⋱

While Victoria was thrilled to read the *Halapid* newsletter, rather than drawing closer to Judaism, she is now involved with a "temple" that is part of the Messianic Movement in the United States. These temples conduct Christian services within the form of Jewish ritual.

When I first heard of her involvement, I tried to keep an open mind. After all, the church our cousins had attended in Los Angeles tried to model itself on the early Christian communities, with a set of families who kept the church going on a communal basis.

Victoria says that there are other families like ours — Mexican

Christians of Jewish heritage — who attend these Messianic services, and they study Hebrew. She gave me some magazines from one of the organizations affiliated with these temples. I leafed through it, puzzled by the combination of political and religious content.

"Is the purpose of this congregation to convert Jews to Christianity?" I asked.

"Yes!" she answered. "They need to see that Jesus is the true Messiah."

At the same time, picking up on the stories of a rabbi or two in the family, Victoria and her son decided that we are descended from the House of David. I tried to explain that the title *rabbi* or *reb* meant "teacher," and could be held by anyone who was a religious teacher. From research that our oldest cousin did, we understand that our ancestors were allied with a famous bandit in northern Spain, Roque Guinart, so it seems unlikely that they were strictly religious, or that any bloodlines to King David were preserved. Victoria and her son began to call my parents' modest retirement house, which has since been sold, "*la estancia*," the estate. Her son painted pictures of it, a typical California rambler, with the coat of arms in the corner of the painting. My father, who never gets his equally ancient coat of arms painted, seems to take this with good humor.

I am not sure how Victoria described her enthusiasm for this approach to religion to my cousins in Los Angeles, but they were uninterested to the point of hostility.

"They don't want to talk about it," she says. "They say they're not Jewish."

"They're not," I said. "They're Christian."

"So are we!" she says. "But our ancestors were Jews."

"Right," I said. "Exactly."

"But don't you think that's interesting?"

"Well, I wrote a book about it," I say.

"Oh, yes!" she said. "Of course."

There is an awkward pause. I sense that Victoria wants some sort of validation for what she is doing that no one else in the family will give her. Something about using our own ancestry to coerce others out of their religion seems to offend the rest of us. After all, they kept the faith, and we did not. Is this some sort of guilt thing that we have to carry around with us? Our ancestors chose life. But something about Victoria's approach rings false.

Seth D. Kunin, Dean of Arts and Humanities at the University of

Dunham, U.K., wrote a paper called "Juggling Identities among the Crypto-Jews of the American Southwest."[1]

In it, he applies concepts from structuralism as defined by the anthropologist Claude Lévi-Strauss to the phenomenon of crypto-Judaism, setting up four "ideal types" of crypto-Jews, depending on four components: self-identification as Jews, practices, genealogy, and beliefs. Generally speaking, our family falls into the second category, "individuals with a Jewish identity but with more ambiguous expressions of the other elements." Kunin also points out that these categories are fluid, and individuals can move back and forth across them, depending on their knowledge, their practice, and their beliefs. Most of the Messianics fall into the fourth category, with no documented genealogy or traditions of Jewish origins, but who "feel" themselves to be Jewish.

"This is all your fault," my husband says.

"Why? I didn't start it."

"No, but you wrote about it."

Two years ago I met a distant relative on the East Coast who has also taken up with the Messianics, and follows a Latino preacher within the movement. She visited Saltillo, perhaps looked up our relatives there. Historically, the Catholic relatives in Saltillo have seen it all, and were probably not fazed. If any of them are practicing Jews, all the more reason to keep it a secret.

Different members of the family have drawn closer to Judaism, and one first cousin even attended a synagogue in Texas briefly. One relative converted to Judaism in order to marry, but had been unaware of his Jewish ancestry. More recently, I have heard from relatives who never lost that connection and are now Orthodox Jews.

II

On one level, one can coolly research history, listen to family stories, and pick out elements that spark the imagination and work in a novel. On another level, I often have to stop and cry. Why am I crying? For things that are lost: family, dignity, connections. Perhaps I cry for my grandfather sent away by his mother, spending the night alone in a train station before resolving to make his new religion his life.

"23rd September, 1895: I left Saltillo at ten in the night with a heavy heart. Just as the train pulled away, I saw between the shadows the silhouette of the mountains of my city of birth, from which I left like a displaced person, cast out by my own because of Evangelism. . . . In the middle of the night I was alone in the station at Garcia. Raising my soul to God, I prayed for divine direction."[2]

Had she ignored his conversion, treated it as a youthful impulse, he might have let it slip away and accepted his place in Catholic Mexican society.

But that has never been the way of the Narros. Stubborn, taciturn, maddeningly sure of our own righteousness, we have often been the loners in a crowd. To our credit, we have also fought injustice on behalf of others, volunteering for churches and charities with the time we could have spent bettering our material lot.

"Ye are the salt of the earth," my Uncle Miguel, his father's namesake, was fond of quoting from the New Testament. "A peculiar people."

And peculiar we were. My grandfather was ordained as a Methodist and died in 1955, a few months after my birth. But really, we practiced a family religion far more restrictive and unforgiving than the Christian methods delineated by John Wesley. This set us apart from the Mexican Catholic community, where social life and religion are so closely intertwined that they cannot be distinguished.

Most of our cousins attended a Protestant church in Los Angeles where they made up the majority of the congregation. My uncles were among the elders, and my cousin led the choir. For a while, the services were held in the basement of a Russian Pentecostal church, and we children used to sneak up the stairs to try to glimpse people falling into trances or speaking in tongues. Those charismatic practices were considered too emotional, too uncontrolled, for us. There were no crosses before our congregation, no vestments on the minister. We sat on metal folding chairs. Singing was the one emotional outlet tolerated, and the church did have a great choir.

Control was the key to religion for us — of the older over the younger, of men over women, of my grandfather over all of us from beyond the grave. I think it is significant that none of his sons followed his lead into the ministry. One of his daughters, Rosa Fe, married a runaway Basque Jesuit from Spain and became a missionary. She wrote and self-published two books, *I Married a Priest*,[3] which was autobiographical, and *Sigrid Marries a Catholic*,[4] which I presume was a cautionary tale.

In San Bernardino, my mother enforced this approach with zeal.

Finding the Spanish-speaking churches not strict enough for her, or requiring baptism by immersion or some other practice that did not suit her, she herded us into Faith Bible Church, a four-square evangelical Protestant church, which wasn't pleased to have a pew taken up by a family of Mexicans. Fortunately, I made friends with another unwilling attendee, a Nez Percé girl as dark and skinny as me who, with her sister, had been adopted by an older white couple. We pushed the limits of how disruptive we could be without getting kicked out of the services.

The really scary part was that you couldn't ask questions in Sunday school. How could we be made in God's image if he is eternal and we are not? Is God a man? Who wrote the Bible? How do we really know that Jesus is the Messiah? The adults who led our classes had been raised in the same faith, which avoided Bible commentaries, since everything we needed was contained in the scriptures themselves. They were expected to answer our questions simply by reading the Bible and quoting it back to us. They stood before us, baffled and annoyed by our curiosity. But the superintendent of Sunday school was a terrifying woman of formidable strength. Although short in stature, she could grip you by the elbow and make you agree to anything just so she would let go. We called her The Little Dictator. In this way, we were cowed into being good Christians.

Our cousins' congregation in Los Angeles purchased its own building—a church gutted by fire—by the time I was a teenager and lovingly restored the interior. They hired an Argentine pastor of Russian origin who was very popular until it was discovered that he was embezzling the church money. By the time I was in my twenties, most of our relatives had drifted away from that church—one aunt and uncle to a new evangelical church that used electric guitars in the service in order to attract young people, one cousin and his wife to the Nazarenes.

I stayed away from church most of my adult life, while my sisters both continued to attend. But the questions I was not allowed to ask in Sunday school continued to haunt me, propelling me into churches and bookstores, where I picked up as many Jewish texts as Christian. As I researched my stories, and then my first novel, the story of my grandfather's conversion and his family's history came to make more sense.

My grandfather came of age during the years before the Mexican Revolution, when the suffering of the landless poor, often displaced from the countryside to the city, could not be ignored, and the vice and corruption of the government under Porfírio Díaz colored any political or social aspirations a young man in Mexico might have had. Though my grandfather's family was not terribly wealthy, they were on the "have" side of the equation. Despite his father's wandering ways, which made my great-grandmother essentially a single parent, my grandfather was given a top-notch education and all of the privileges and responsibilities of an upper-class Mexican citizen.

Yet there was a hole in my grandfather's heart that was only filled by his conversion. His journal tells of the hours after he told his mother of his decision to become a Protestant, spending the night alone in the Saltillo train station, crying and praying. The next day, he took a train to Chihuahua and eventually to Arizona to live with an uncle who had already converted, and joined the ministry.

Eventually, I came to see my grandfather's rejection not only as an act of adolescent rebellion, but as an act of revolution. Miguel Narro was only seventeen when he left the Church, but it was a decision about which he never expressed regret.

By turning his back on Catholicism, and the fatalism he saw it engender, he cast his lot with the poor. The churches he started consisted of a small group of families who would meet in each other's homes for prayer meetings. They would then pool their resources to construct a church building, hire a pastor, and lend emotional, spiritual, and financial support to each other. Once the building was in place, they could attract more members and begin to serve the needs of the wider community. In later years, this approach would be called liberation theology — the idea that the power of the church lay with the people, rather than the institution — but at that time, it was simply the way Protestant churches were established.

In some cases, such as in Guaymas, my grandfather supervised and participated in the construction of the building. He often conducted special "Temperance" services at which people were encouraged to foreswear drinking, a huge economic drain on poor people at the beginning of the twentieth century, and embrace Christianity. He kept exhaustive lists of the attendees at these services, sometimes including their Mexican town of origin. This might have been the way he documented his activities to the American Methodist Church that helped support him.

My grandparents lived all over Northern Mexico and parts of the Southwest, from White Oaks, New Mexico, to Guaymas. They spent a long time in San Antonio, Texas, where my mother received most of her schooling. No one ever says what my grandmother thought about this, but she seems to have carried on with equanimity, bearing eleven children along the way. In marrying my grandmother, an illegitimate orphan of mixed blood, my grandfather solidified his stand with the disenfranchised of this world. Whether or not his Jewish heritage was a factor in my grandfather's conversion, I cannot say. But positioning himself as an outsider seemed to suit him. At one point, after he was married and had children, his mother, Eleuteria Valdés Narro, came to visit, bearing expensive gifts for the children. She offered to write him back into her will if he would give up his religious vocation, but he declined.

My mother and her brothers and sisters grew up in rented houses, with few belongings that they could call their own, mostly cast-off furniture from other people. They slept three to a bed. But my grandfather loved books, and managed to keep a few with him through their many moves. His final assignment was in Los Angeles, where the family purchased a house on Dozier Street that was always after referred to as "The Dozier" and where my grandparents lived until their retirement. They are buried at the cemetery down Brooklyn Avenue, now called Martin Luther King Way.

Rather than joy and exaltation, however, the sort of lifting of a burden one might expect from such idealism, these family stories are accompanied by a sadness that permeates the retellings, lingers over family gatherings like a melancholy fog. The first time I encountered this as an artistic expression was as a college student, when I saw the movie *The Garden of the Finzi-Continis*,[5] about an upper-class Jewish family in Italy at the outbreak of World War II. The best word for it I have come across is in Portuguese, *saudade*, meaning a sort of beautiful nostalgia that one hears in Portuguese music.

I dragged my parents to the movie. In spite of their disapproval of most religions, including the colorful variety of Christian and quasi-Christian sects in Southern California, they especially liked our Jewish friends. My father was a convert from Catholicism to Protestantism, and considered my mother's background an asset.

"Are you Jewish?" they eagerly asked new visitors, sending most of them into paroxysms of embarrassment, Jewish or not. Those who were probably expected to be kicked out of the house, but were, instead, embraced with enthusiasm for all the stereotypes that were usually portrayed as negative. In the movie, I had recognized something of this yearning for things from an idealized past, of paradise lost, of trying to connect with something of which we were no longer a part, even to the point of ignoring the reality around us.

In high school, I briefly dated a young man from across town, a blonde, blue-eyed type with an IQ to match my own. In fact, we had the two highest IQs in the school system, which set all the teachers tittering when they saw us together. We were at his house, listening to music on a record player, when he went into the next room. I heard his father ask what my background was.

"She's Italian," I heard him say.

I went numb, but said nothing. Later, I wondered if I should have walked in and said I was Mexican. When I got up the courage, perhaps two weeks later, I asked why he had said that.

"My father is very conservative," he said. "He would have made you leave. He hates Jews, too."

We broke up shortly after, so I never saw his father again. That was just one glimpse into the minefield that lay ahead of me, and it should have taught me caution. California is a place where looks are important, ethnicity is important, and people sometimes reinvent themselves. I did not try to hide my obvious Mexican identity, but I did not often speak of my Jewish identity, either. Besides, I still did not really understand it, that great mystery—how could one be Mexican and Jewish at the same time? Christian and Jewish? What does it mean to be Jewish? I still wonder.

The summer I turned ten, I decided to read all of the Bible. I finished the Old Testament, even all the begats, in a sort of white-hot heat that I would recognize later as the effect that a really good idea has on me as a writer. I felt transformed, enlightened in a way that I had never felt before.

I told my mother that I wished we were Jewish.

"He made a Covenant with Noah that he would always protect them," I told her.

"But we are Jewish!" she said.

This was the first time I remember hearing this. "But then why don't we keep the Laws?"

"We follow the teachings of Christ in the New Testament."

"But then we're Christian, not Jewish."

"We are Christian! The people who came before us were Jewish. Our ancestors."

This really confused me. "But why did we become Christian if we were already Jewish? Isn't Holly Jewish?" Holly was my best friend.

"Yes, but we are Christian now because we believe in Jesus."

Even then, I could sense that something was being left out, but I would not find out what it was for another twenty years or more.

"Read all of the New Testament," she said. "Then you will understand why we are Christian. Jesus said to give up the old laws for the new. And the new ones are the Ten Commandments."

I tried to read the New Testament, I really did. But it was very repetitive. The first several books tell the same story about Jesus several times instead of telling new stories about different people. And the relationship with God was much more distant. Nobody lived to be nine hundred years old or walked with God.

The last part of the New Testament is the book of Revelations by the Apostle John, and it is full of weird, hallucinatory images. This book is very popular with Evangelicals, because one can read all sorts of things into it. For example, in my family, the allusions to the great whore of Babylon are obviously to the Roman Catholic Church.

Over the next year, I began to pepper Holly with questions. Her family, especially her father, was not especially religious, so she knew less than I did. This interest culminated in her mother inviting me over to celebrate seder one year, the first they had observed in a long time. I tasted the bitter and the sweet. I placed a cup of wine to my lips, something my mother, who was virulently opposed to drinking, would have considered evil.

At some point, I thanked Holly's family for inviting me, and her father got up and left the table in disgust.

"It's okay," said her mother. "He really doesn't like anything having to do with religion. But I have wanted to do this for a long time."

I did not convert at that time, since no one offered me the opportunity — not that my mother would have allowed it — but the seed of doubt was planted. Over the years, I was strongly attracted to Judaism, but failed to make the move.

I seem to be stranded with my family at this intersection of culture and religion — too Mexican to be Protestant, too Protestant to be Jewish, and too Jewish to be Mexican — from which various individuals make forays out in different directions.

Søren Kierkegaard, the Danish philosopher, wrote about religion as the last and most difficult step to take in the development of a mature person. It required a "leap of faith," one the unnamed narrator of his book, *Fear and Trembling*, was himself unable to take. A Web site about Kierkegaard says, "In addition to being dubbed 'the father of existentialism,' Kierkegaard is best known as a trenchant critic of Hegel and Hegelianism and for his invention or elaboration of a host of philosophical, psychological, literary and theological categories, including: anxiety, despair, melancholy, repetition, inwardness, irony, existential stages, inherited sin, teleological suspension of the ethical, Christian paradox, the absurd, reduplication, universal/exception, sacrifice, love as a duty, seduction, the demonic, and indirect communication."[6]

Wait, that all sounds like me! Maybe I should become a Dane! No, wait, then I would have to learn Danish. Like Kierkegaard's narrator, I probably just think too much.

There is a certain uneasiness between the Ashkenazi Jews and the Sephardic Jews that affects the already-tenuous standing of the crypto-Jews, something more than a difference in languages, food, and the form of the religious service. Victor Perera, whose family emigrated from Israel to Guatemala, addressed this in his memoir, *The Cross and the Pear Tree*.[7] Perera taught journalism at the University of California Berkeley before his premature death, in 2003. He spent his life trying to address injustice, including the treatment of non-Ashkenazic Jews in Israel. This difference in standing between the North African/Mediterranean/Latin Jews and the Northern European Ashkenazi Jews seems to be the subtext to many of the current arguments against the continued existence of crypto-Jews. Besides anecdotal evidence, research such as that published in 2002 by Janet Liebman Jacobs, *Hidden Heritage: The Legacy of the Crypto-Jews*, argues for our existence.[8]

∴ ∴ ∴ ∴ ∴

When I was two, my family took me to visit Saltillo. These are my very first memories. One is of wrapping my hands around the whorls of a wrought-iron gate and peering into a lush garden with a fountain at its center. I understood that it had belonged to our family, but we could never enter it. My grandfather was cast out of the Garden of Eden to make his way in the world. For some reason, my family has identified that idyllic time not with our immediate Catholic ancestors, or even with our living relatives there, but with our more elusive, Jewish ones.

And so this has come to be a central metaphor in my stories — the beautiful but neglected garden, the fountain, the world for which we yearn, but to which we can never return. And in my stories, that garden belongs to a Jewish family — one that has kept the faith. I sometimes wonder what our lives would be like if my grandfather, rather than being befriended by a Protestant family in Michigan, had been taken in by a Jewish one. Would we, his descendants, have been accepted? Or simply marginalized again?

By that fountain, I like to imagine, members of my family would recognize each other and embrace. Friends would come forward and say that they had been waiting for us all this time. Perhaps the missing resolution to the family stories will come when I am finally able to push open that garden gate and step inside.

A Thread in the Tapestry

The Narros of Saltillo, Mexico, in History

and Literature

My first novel, *Spirits of the Ordinary*, is based on the story of my maternal great-grandparents, Pablo Narro Narro and Eleuteria Valdés Rodriguez. My great-grandfather had the gold fever and was wasting the family's resources prospecting for gold. My maternal great-grandmother was able to cut him off financially. I had always wondered about this relationship and the status of women in Mexico at this time, around the 1870s. At the same time, I began my research into the Jews of Mexico. I researched in my uncle's private library in Chihuahua, Mexico, at the Institute of Texas Cultures in San Antonio, Texas, at the Amerind Foundation in Dragoon, Arizona, and in various libraries and archives in Mexico City.

I ended up writing three novels spanning the era of the Porfiriato, from around 1870 to the early 1900s, when Porfírio Díaz was president of Mexico.

During the 1970s and '80s, my Uncle Miguel Narro, and later his son, Miguel Narro, began inquiring in earnest after our family roots. My cousin eventually commissioned a family tree from a researcher in Saltillo, confirming the origin of the family in a town called Nyer. It is on the French side of the border between France and Spain, just east of the principality of Andorra. According to this research, the original family name was Niarro, and they spent their time feuding with a family called the Cadells. The town of Nyer was under the protection of the Banyuls family, and there is to this day a stone castle at the site. This is in accord with the Narro family crest, which is "*de oro, con un castillo de piedra, al natural, cantonado de cuatro estrellas de azur*" — of gold, with a castle of stone, natural colored, surrounded by four blue stars — four six-pointed blue stars.[1]

Not until I began writing my novels in the early 1990s did I take a real interest in the family history. In the University of Washington library, I found the book by Robles.[2] It contained an entire chapter on the Jews of Saltillo, including the story of Governor Luís Carvajál, the governor of the province whose family was persecuted for being practicing Jews. The governor was exposed in part by the writings and personal confession of his nephew and namesake, who had undergone a profound, personal conversion back to Judaism, and wrote under the pseudonym of Iosef Lumbroso (1567–1596). Six other members of the governor's family were also executed in 1596, and the family continued to be persecuted for many years after.

In 1991, while researching an article for a new magazine I had helped establish, *The Raven Chronicles*, I met an elder in Seattle named Isaac Maimon. I called him after seeing an article in the paper about the five-hundredth anniversary of the Spanish Diaspora. I interviewed him for the magazine,[3] and found that he had photos and documentation on the Sephardim in Seattle. We met in the dining room of his home while his wife, Esther, baked sweet pastries in the adjacent kitchen.

Maimon was born in Turkey in 1913, and came with his family to the Northwest during the fall of the Ottoman Empire. His father was the first Sephardic rabbi in Seattle, which had the third-largest Sephardic population in the United States, he said. Retired from the grocery business, Maimon gave classes in Ladino at his synagogue.

I recounted my surprise at first hearing Ladino on the radio, how natural and comprehensible it seemed, and mentioned our family stories. Suddenly, Isaac Maimon was interviewing me. Does your family light candles on Friday nights? He asked. Play cards? Use biblical first names? No, no and yes, as far as I knew. I explained the conversion in the late 1800s, the aversion to eating pork, to all religious ritual, especially the wearing of crucifixes or their display in church.

Maimon, who attended conferences all over the world on Sephardic affairs, was not surprised. Nor was he surprised by the lack of verifiable evidence. "The point was to remain hidden," he said. "In preparation for the quincentennial of the Diaspora, Jews all over the world were asked to participate. People in Spain, everywhere, pulled menorahs out of their basements. Only the Jews of Northern Mexico and New Mexico refused. They said they were comfortable the way they were."

I thought of the flagellants on holy days in New Mexico, who always reminded me of the KKK, and understood perfectly. In an isolated town, who would protect you?

This was the first time that I understood the direct connection between the Spanish Inquisition and my family. This was the first time that I understood the meaning of many of the stories that had been told, quietly but urgently, over the years. It was the first time that I realized that my family was not an anomaly, an isolated event in time. We were one of many.

Still, the fact that our branch of the family was now Protestant seemed to further set us apart from our ancestors. When my grandfather Miguel was seventeen, he was sent to Michigan to study English in preparation for college, intending to study mechanical engineering. Instead, he was befriended by a family who encouraged his conversion from Catholicism to Protestantism. He was subsequently disinherited and excommunicated by his family. At that time, 1894, he went to live and work with his uncle, Enríque Narro, in Tucson, Arizona. There he met and married my grandmother, Rosa Martinez, shortly after her fifteenth birthday. They went on to have twelve children. My mother, Lydia Narro, was born in 1916 in Durango, Mexico.

Because of the conversion, many of the traditions associated with Catholicism had been left behind as superstitious or idolatrous. My family did not drink, smoke, dance, or play cards. Although steeped in religion, we did not wear crosses. The worship services of my relatives did not have crosses in front of the church and were organized along the lines of the early Christians, with elders giving the sermons or serving the communion. Mostly, we did not eat pork, but I understood that to be for health reasons.

In early 2000, I saw a documentary called *Expulsion and Memory: Descendants of the Hidden Jews*[4] in which Dr. Tomás Atencio said that his father had been a Presbyterian minister and showed a menorah carved into the foundation of one of the churches in which his father worked. Dr. Atencio went on to say that many crypto-Jews converted to Protestantism when the missionaries came to the area around the turn of the century because it offered access to the scriptures, something not possible under pre–Vatican II Catholicism. All of this time, most crypto-Judaic practices had been perpetuated almost purely through memory.

The Jewish identity would explain why my family might reside in a French border town for three hundred years and manage to retain a distinct identity. But I was still puzzled about their immigration to Mexico. Although it was two hundred years after the worst of the Inquisition in Mexico, it was still an oppressively Catholic country. I have come up with two possible explanations. The two brothers Narro are supposed to have immigrated in the late 1700s. This would have been shortly after the French Revolution, which took place in 1789. The first explanation is that things had been going well for the family and took a turn for the worse after the Revolution, prompting them to flee. The second possible explanation is that, in 1791, the newly Republican French government, for the first time, granted full rights of citizenship to its Jewish inhabitants. At the same time, the Bourbon reforms in Spain began to encourage new economic growth in her colonies, and by 1800, Mexico's economy was booming. Other than highway robbery, there probably was not a lot going on, economically, in the Pyrenees. This combination of circumstances may have induced the Narros to make the journey across the Atlantic to an existing Jewish community in Saltillo.

❖ ❖ ❖ ❖ ❖

Later, I made a few inquiries into our family's genealogy. I posted a message on FamilyHistory.com asking for stories about the Narros. I heard from three people, one also seeking information, and two with a little. One was a young man from Saltillo who was in Oregon as an exchange student. His name was Felipe Narro Monsiváis, and he had the same general information that I had about Jewish ancestors and our relationship to Manuel Acuña, a famous poet. The third person, Albert Villegas, a resident of Plano, Texas, had done extensive genealogical research. He was able to confirm our relationship through his great ×6 grandfather, and my great ×5 grandfather, Juan José Francisco Alonso Narro Martínez Guajardo. He confirms our ancestors as Conversos, but has few family stories. Ben Nahman's Web site lists *Narro* as a Sephardic name.[5] My oldest sister, who has visited Spain several times, has been told that the name was sometimes used as a pseudonym by Jews who changed their names from more overtly Jewish names. When I visited Mexico

City in 1998, I found 17 Narros or Narro-Garcias in the phone book. I was told by a Catholic family that the Narros they knew were Jewish.

Every Narro I or my immediate relatives have met can be traced back to Saltillo, including the child of an American sailor stationed in Scotland during World War II. The Narros were, until recently, closely intermarried, in keeping with the colonial patterns of Northern Mexico, Texas, and New Mexico. As times have changed, members of my family have begun to talk more openly about our Jewish heritage, and some of the women wear Stars of David. One of my male cousins also attended temple in El Paso, Texas, for a time, but did not convert. I have only confirmed one conversion back to Judaism, by a young cousin once removed who married a Jew. But I don't think he was aware of his Jewish heritage at the time. I have also heard from relatives whose families never gave up the practice of Judaism, and now practice openly. The connection is strong enough to have endured through all of these centuries and two religious changes. Today, there are Narros in twenty of the United States, over half of them in Texas.

It was with great sadness that I read an article in the *Atlantic Monthly*[6] that discounted the evidence of crypto-Judaic heritage in New Mexico. I think that my own research, independent of any larger movement or personal agenda, offers plenty of proof that these communities have existed, do exist, and will continue to flourish. The Narros are just one thread in the wider community of Hispanics of Jewish heritage. Because the name is distinct, and the family is well documented in Saltillo, with an agricultural college named after it, as well as several writers and artists of note, the Narros offer a window onto the past that supports the research and family stories of many others.

Presented to the Society for Crypto-Judaic Studies
Pueblo, Colorado
August 21, 2001

Unveiling the Spirits

Since my presentation of two years ago in Pueblo, Colorado, called "A Thread in the Tapestry: The Narros of Saltillo, Mexico, in History and Literature," I was given the opportunity to travel to Saltillo in April 2002, when I spoke at the University of Texas–Pan American, in Edinburg. I delayed my return flight and took a bus to Saltillo. After arriving very late, I got up the next morning and began walking around the city. One of the primary tourist attractions is the Sarapes de Saltillo shop, where the famous sarapes with the star-shaped design are still woven by hand. I stopped to photograph the retired proprietor, Ana María Oyarzábalde Mendoza, who was sitting in the entranceway with her son, who has Down's syndrome. They still greet customers as they come in, although the señora's daughter now runs the business. I asked permission to photograph her, and spoke briefly with her daughter. She told me that there were Narros living next door.

There, I met Manuel Moreira y Narro and his sister, Amalia Moreira Narro de Heede. They had time to talk and knew a lot about the family history. They told me that a book had been commissioned from a researcher named Marta Durón, who lives in Aguascalientes and is married into the Narro family.[1] Along with original research, she compiled genealogies, photographs, and family stories from several branches of the family. It includes an excerpt from book 2, chapter 60 of the novel *Don Quixote de la Mancha*, by Miguel de Cervantes Saavedra, describing an encounter with Roque Guinart, a notorious leader in the feud between the Niarros and Cadells. "These thieves are under the direction of Roque Guinart, who turns out to be a dignified man with a well-intentioned, albeit warped, ethical sense,"[2] according to one summary. Guinart escorts Quixote and Sancho Panza to the outskirts of Barcelona, but his territory was in the Pyrenees in a region that is now part of France. I was able to obtain a copy of the Narro book, which contains three hundred pages of materials. A copy is also now in the collection of the University of Texas–Pan American, where the special collections librarian, George Gause, had been aware of the existence of the book and was delighted to obtain a copy.

Since that visit, I discovered that my grandfather was born in the building that is now the Sarapes de Saltillo shop. I have also heard from a number of relatives who came across "A Thread in the Tapestry" on the *Halapid*[3] Web site. They live in places as far-flung as New York City and Tampico, Mexico.

I asked Amalia and Miguel about our supposed Jewish ancestry, and they readily admitted that it was considered common knowledge. In their case, both sides of the family can be traced to Jewish origin, they said, since their father is of Portuguese lineage. In that part of Mexico, at least, anyone who was originally Portuguese is assumed to have been Jewish, as well. They said that the Spaniards of "good blood" were given the rich land, the silver mines to the west, and the Jews ended up with the poor land, suitable primarily for raising cattle. However, there is no mention of our Jewish ancestry in the book of family history, and the updated versions of Vito Alessio Robles's history of Saltillo[4] no longer contain the chapter on the Jews of Saltillo. All the Jews have disappeared from the currently available histories, along with any mention of the unfortunate Carvajál family. The city recently celebrated 425 years since its founding.

Spirits of the Ordinary

In June of 2002, José Eduardo González, executive artistic director of the Miracle Theatre of Portland, Oregon, asked Olga Sánchez and me to adapt my novel, *Spirits of the Ordinary*, for the stage. Olga would direct the production. There were two staged readings with audience feedback, one in Seattle and one in Portland, as well as many, many rewrites. Because the novel has many characters and settings, the original plot was pared down so that it could be performed by ten actors playing multiple parts on a small stage. Many of our favorite characters fell by the wayside, and the focus that emerged was on Julio's relationship with his wayward son, Zacarías. Zacarías, based on my great-grandfather, Pablo Narro, shuns his father's mystical explorations of the Jewish scriptures, preferring to hunt for gold instead.

The play was staged during May 2003, closing the season for the Miracle Theatre. Because the situations of actors on a stage need to be self-explanatory, much of the narrative exposition available to the novelist was removed. Instead, through the addition of choreography and music, the play took on powerful emotional strength. While some actors played the characters, others acted as a sort of veiled chorus to echo and emphasize the words. This heightened the mystical quality of the play, but also tied it to the forces of nature that are so important.

The chapter that had been called "Noche Lluviosa" was changed to a secret Passover scene, showing Julio and Mariana celebrating a crypto-Jewish seder in their home while Zacarías is out in the desert looking for gold. Julio and Mariana describe themselves in third person through the use of transcripts from The Inquisitorial records. Language was also added showing how they made do with the foods and materials available to them.

Some of the language is taken from David M. Gitlitz's *Secrecy and Deceit: The Religion of the Crypto-Jews*,[1] as well as Jewish practices around Monterrey as described in *Los judíos bajo la inquisición en hispanoamérica*, by Boleslao Lewin.[2] In addition, I discovered that actors have a lot to say about a play, and language and details were added that originated with them.

Excerpt from the play, *Spirits of the Ordinary*[3]

act 1, scene 13

At night. Thunder and flashes of lightning. ARMADIO *and* CARRANZA *are walking on patrol.*

ARMADIO: That was a loud one. What a crack! I won't stay out much longer, doctor. I doubt there's any trouble tonight and I don't much feel like getting soaked. Not good for the health, is it?

CARRANZA: You're absolutely right, Colonel.

ARMADIO: Nothing happens in this town. A blessing and a curse.

Lightning and thunder.

ARMADIO: Ay, hombre, the devil never sleeps! Time to go inside.

They exit. It begins to rain heavily. JULIO *and* MARIANA *hang coverings on the inside of their windows, then candles are lit.* JULIO *and* MARIANA *are seen celebrating Passover, standing. They are wearing traveling clothes, and holding staffs.* OLD MAN *and* OLD WOMAN *spirits look on.*

JULIO: In the spring, on a certain day she does not remember, but last year it was Holy Thursday, she was to observe a fast called the Feast of the Lamb, not eating or drinking the entire day. And after this fast she was to celebrate the Passover that lasted for seven days. And then she should slaughter a lamb which was to be roasted whole, and to invite all her relatives to the feast. (MARIANA *laughs.*)

The bones were to be burned, which commemorated the sacrifice of the law of Moses. And on those seven days she had to eat unleavened bread, nor could she have any leaven in the house. And she was to prepare little flat cakes on new brick, and to cook them on the fire, and these were to be distributed among her relatives.

MARIANA: Why would they only have unleavened bread?

JULIO: When they were told to go they went, with what bread they could make quickly.

MARIANA: And a hard boiled egg, and cilantro.

In another part of the stage, ZACARÍAS *enters with La Gata.*

ZACARÍAS: Sssh. Venga, Gata. Perhaps this rain has driven everyone away. Or perhaps the military? Ssh. Nothing, not even the usual 'Trespassers Will Be Shot' sign. Esmeralda, why have you been abandoned?

MARIANA: Seder participants stood, booted, their sticks in their hands, in literal fulfillment of the Biblical precept.

JULIO: They had no Haggadah, but read the Exodus story directly from the Catholic Vulgate. As we do.

ZACARÍAS: Pieces of equipment, crushed wagons, scattered everywhere. Some kind of avalanche, no human force could cause this kind of destruction. The earth itself looks forsaken. Ugh. (*He has a stomach pang.*)

MARIANA: I will sing to the Lord, for He has triumphed gloriously; Horse and driver he has hurled into the sea.

ZACARÍAS: God, I feel terrible. Next time, only clean water. Only drink clean water . . . I don't have any more time for mistakes.

JULIO: Who is like you, Oh Lord, among the celestials,
Awesome in splendor, working wonders!
You put out your right hand, The earth swallowed them,
In your love you lead the people you redeemed,
In Your strength you guide them to Your holy abode.
The people hear, they tremble;
Agony grips the dwellers in Philistia.

MARIANA: Sing to the Lord, for He has triumphed gloriously; Horse and driver he has hurled into the sea.

ZACARÍAS: What's this? Here, Gata, let's duck in here. (*He stoops as though entering a cave.*) Ah, a little dry ground! Must be an old mine shaft. So tight. (*He sets up a lantern and starts to make camp, then stops and picks up a rock.*) What's this? Gold!

There's gold in here! Gold for the taking, Gata! I just reached out my hand and it's lying on the ground . . . my little hammer? (*He pulls out his pick and begins digging feverishly.*)

JULIO: A lamb has to be cooked whole and you have to eat it standing up, without damaging a single bone of the lamb.

ZACARÍAS: Deeper, deeper. Ah, the air is so thick, wet. (*He ties his bandana around his forehead, empties his supplies out of a bag and begins filling it with rocks.*) Esmeralda, you sweet thing!

MARIANA: Lamb with bitter lettuce, and unleavened bread.

ZACARÍAS: My fingers are bloody. My beauty, I want to look at you in the light. All things in their time. (*He lifts his pack.*) Uhn, 120 pounds at least. More than enough to pay what I've borrowed. (*He pushes, pulls, carries, drags the bag out of the mine. We hear other voices, the sound of men approaching on horseback.*)

JULIO: Where are you taking us, Moses?
Here in this desert place
Where there is no bread
Nor firewood
Nor pasturage nor cattle?

ZACARÍAS: One more push, come on, one more . . .

MARIANA: In honor and praise of the holy names of the Lord!
In remembrance of our brothers, when they left Egypt and entered the Promised Land.

JULIO: Amen. (*They set aside their staffs and sit down at the table.*)

MINING CAPTAIN: There! Ladrón! This is private property! (*Shots are fired.*)

ZACARÍAS: Gata! Where are you? (*He tries to lift the pack to carry with him but after his exertion, it is too heavy. He empties it as quickly as he can, until it is light enough for him to run. He trips and falls, but gets up, holding his neck, and manages to escape the gunfire.*)

JULIO: What would our ancestors think of us? Celebrating the Phase (*fa-say*) with tortillas?

MARIANA: They are unleavened. They are wrapped in new cloth. As they did for forty years in the wilderness, we do what we can.

MINING CAPTAIN: Thief! This is private property! Show yourself! (*More shots fired.*)

JULIO: And where do you think he is, tonight? In the old days, a prophet might go into the desert for forty days and have a vision. But what did they have to contend with in the old days? Slavery. A few Hittites, the Philistines. A Pharaoh here and there. Surely not the Apaches. Surely not La Guardia. *Definitely* not the Texas Rangers, if he wanders that far north! If only we knew where he was.

MARIANA: Sometimes they must go away before they return.

JULIO: Will he return? In one piece? I am afraid our son has fallen into the *kelipot*, the realm of evil. I can't see him! Of what use are all my years of study? All my work?

MARIANA: He is here, with us, in spirit. Drink, Julio.

JULIO: Blessed are Thou, O Lord our God, Ruler of the Universe, who has created the fruit of the vine. (*They both drink.*)

Sound of hoofbeats and gunshots.

Presented to the Society for Crypto-Judaic Studies
San Antonio, Texas
August 4, 2003

❖ IV ❖
Found in Translation

Found in Translation

I was born the youngest in a Spanish-speaking household. My parents and aunts and uncles spoke Spanish, and we, the children, listened. As my two older sisters went to school and brought home English, I heard more English than the others, and gradually, less Spanish. It was said that my early language had a Basque accent, because my uncle, a runaway Basque Jesuit priest who married my aunt, talked a lot. No one said whether my accent was in English or in Spanish. It didn't matter, and we didn't remember, because the languages were interchangeable.

As I grew older and tried to analyze my relationship with language, I realized that I had spent most of my life translating. I processed the Spanish in which I was addressed into the images in my head, and answered in English, because that was the language in which I was educated, starting at the age of five. Before entering school, I don't think I was expected to answer, only listen. At the same time, I was trying to understand what was expected of me at school and translate that into what I had been taught at home. I was considered shy, at first, because I would not look an adult in the eye. In college, I was horrified to find that I was expected to address my professors by their first names, and mostly didn't address them by name at all. I don't think I even knew my parents had first names until I was a teenager.

I survived the traumas of young adulthood, but just barely. Add to the usual mix the differences in dating expectations, humor, and the self-image of a young woman — and this in the seventies — and you get the idea. I was not only miserable, but I made those around me miserable. I tried, I really did try, but I had been raised to be a proper young woman comfortably ensconced in Northern Mexico in, say, 1895. That is why it was easy for me to write about nineteenth-century Mexico. I didn't just read about it, I lived it. My mother's father's family — before the Revolution, before my grandfather's conversion and expulsion from the family home — was our point of cultural reference. The intervening years and change in economic and social status, from upper-class landowners to the people near the tracks in Southern California, were incidental.

Much has been lost in translation. In our case, we will always be a subgroup of a subculture — Jews who don't know Hebrew, Indians who don't pray to the morning star. Those of you who have tried to return to the past know that things are irrevocably altered by the passage of time and history. You can go back, but not to what your ancestors, or even a younger self, left behind.

We are misinformed, misunderstood, misled, and mistaken for something else.

"Are you Hawaiian?" people ask me. "Filipina? Finnish?"

No, I answer, my parents are from Mexico. My uncle used to tell people he was an Abyssinian Jew, a concept obscure enough at the time to throw his questioners off long enough for him to make an escape. But behind the questions is a search for connections. We each seek to retrace those steps that led us from where we once were, to where we are now. A familiar-sounding name, the slant of an eye, can evoke the memory of that path in a passing observer.

But I had a special gift. One of my first jobs was in the press office of the Democratic National Committee in Washington, D.C. They used to send me the crank callers, the ones who wanted to talk about the conspiracy in the media between the national parties and the major networks, how it was all a trick to promote consumerism.

"You're right," I would tell them. "We take big money from special interests and buy advertising with it. What are you going to do about it? Do you vote? Are you registered to vote?" Most of them were incredulous that anyone would bother to engage them in dialogue. Some of them even thanked me for being honest.

Later I moved to western Colorado and worked for three counties and a small city — Ouray — to bring in public television from Denver. I had to write the grants, order the equipment, and supervise the construction of an elaborate translator and microwave system. I had no idea what I was doing, but the county commissioners — mostly small-business owners and ranchers, trusted me to explain this stuff to them. Terms like *line of sight* and *height above average terrain* and *footprint* rolled off my tongue as I justified this $300,000 project.

In Seattle, I went to work for the Catholic archdiocese, helping ethnic minority communities to organize and raise funding for their specific projects, often youth related. I would go to a party, or a dinner, or a funeral, where the elders — a tribal chairman, a grandma with knitting in hand — would graciously welcome me as an observer while they discussed the issues at hand. By some miracle of talk, they would resolve differences and reach a consensus without any one person seeming to take the lead. I then returned to the archdiocese to explain how these decisions had been made to a deeply, *steeply*, hierarchical system of men in black.

About six months before my son was born, in 1989, I turned full-time to writing. I had written and published a few short stories, and set out to finish my first book-length collection of work.

I do a lot of research for my writing, and much of it is in Spanish. Over the years, I have learned to read Spanish, and I don't even use a dictionary very much. Usually, it is not the words that trip me up, but the intent: why did the author write this? For example, a few years ago I found an article on the Opata written by a Mexican economist.[1] He kept referring to the indigenous problem. What problem? I could not figure this out. I finally realized that the problem, fifty years after the Mexican Revolution, was that the indigenous people of Sonora don't produce exportable capital. They live a self-sufficient lifestyle in which they grow the food that they eat. Because this does not contribute to a national or international economy, it is considered a problem. This attitude echoed exactly that of *los científicos*, Porfírio Díaz's group of advisors who, in the late 1800s, helped him convert Mexico to a modern economy at the expense of its working people. This was one of the major causes of the Mexican Revolution.

Another example of this sort of decoding of text came in newspaper accounts of that time. I came across an article decrying the large number of women who worked as prostitutes in Paris, and what a shame it was that they could not be educated to do something else for a living. Why should people in Mexico City care about this, I wondered. Then I realized that the article was really about Mexico City, in a roundabout way. Prostitution was a huge problem in Mexico City at the time, many women having been displaced from the countryside and winding up living on the streets. In those days, you could hire a woman to work in a factory for half the daily wage of a man, and a child for one-third the wages of a man. People were desperate, and there were calls almost daily in the paper to include women in the educational system. But Mexico City looked to Paris as the example of what it wanted to be when it grew up — not New York, not London, but Paris. So by discussing the problem in Paris, the writer was really calling attention to the situation in Mexico.

A reverse example of this is time I spent in the town of Te-potzlán, located near Cuernavaca. After spending five days in Mexico City researching, I escaped to Tepotzlán for the Day of the Dead. Here is an excerpt from my journal, about an event in which ancient symbols had been translated for a modern celebration:

> Several of the artists had made an ofrenda, an offering in the shape of an altar, for the Day of the Dead. It was quite beautiful. There were several tiers with candles, and cut-out designs in blue and yellow. On the ground were flat sculptures in sand, of the sort Lázaro Fulgencio, an artist in Seattle, knows how to make. In front of that was the large shape of a valentine made of whole marigold flowers. At first I thought that part of the bottom had been displaced, since it trailed downward in a straight line, and almost moved it back with my foot. Then I realized that it was a stylized bleeding heart. From the rafters over the whole hung tissue paper cut-outs in many colors. In this case, modern artistic representations had been re-imagined to serve an ancient purpose.

∴ ∴ ∴ ∴ ∴

I am a person born not only of translations, but of transitions — my very existence marks that conjunction between one culture and another. By claiming this borderland as my own, by acknowledging that I am neither one nor the other, but both, I have been able to reach out and find the parts of each culture that pertain to me. I will never really understand Mexican politics, or be able to tell a joke in English; but I appreciate the beauty and magic inherent in both languages.

I have come to realize, finally, that my life's work, whatever it has been called, is the act of translation. Not necessarily from one language to another, but between world views. I am a translator between worlds, between cultures, between jargons and contexts. And in trying to explain these many worlds to others and to myself, I have become a writer.

With the translation of my work into Spanish, as well as other languages, I feel that my writing is on its way to coming full circle. For that is how my stories started — told to me in Spanish, and written down to be found in translation.

A Woman Called Concha

I am interested in the big questions: Who are we, and what is our place in the universe? I am interested in writing that connects people to people, people to the land, and people to God.

These are the things I value in language:

- conciseness
- simplicity
- transparency

The first two are self-explanatory. Transparent language is that which acts as a conduit between people and ideas, shuttling the reader as quickly as possible to the image or situation being described, while calling a minimum amount of attention to itself: *A woman lived in the desert.* The opposite of this, language that demands to be acknowledged, pondered, and penetrated, I call opaque language: *Somewhere was water, and somewhere, there wasn't water. Somewhere, there wasn't a woman, and somewhere, there was.*

The irony of this is that concise, simple, transparent language is not always the quickest or most insightful way to a set of ideas. Thus, metaphor and description take their place. The reader must be taken on a journey in order to understand the images presented. The reader must be provided with context. And that context must provide a link between the reader's world and the world within the words created or presented by the writer: *Once, there was a woman who traveled a long, hard way to live in Tucson. We have a photograph of her, and we can imagine her life. Her name was Concha.*

This is best done with great specificity: the more exact the detail, the more complex the ideas the writer is able to convey in a meaningful way: *Concha heard her name and turned. It was her real name,*

her Indian name, Shark's Tooth from the Sea, and it gave back to her
memories of a childhood that she thought she had lost forever.

A good story works like a musical composition. An idea is presented, elaborated, debated and perhaps defeated, and finally, presented to the reader in a modified, more mature form that embodies the path that was traveled in order to reach that idea. By taking the reader on a journey, we, to a certain extent, can re-create in their experience the thought processes and emotions of our characters. This should be done with compassion, humor, and generosity. But again like music, we can provide a pattern, a symmetry and closure that one seldom encounters in life. That is why reading good writing is pleasurable and fulfilling. That is why listening to good music can induce ecstasy.

The writer and her language should be the humble servant of the reader. To me, the act of writing is not fulfilled until it is read. The words need to be read, digested, and assembled within the context of the reader's mind and experiences in order to be complete. In other words, every reader is "reading" a different story, because every reader brings a different set of experiences and sensibilities to the story. The word *desert* might evoke the smell of sage. *Concha* might mean the touch of a work-worn hand. It also means "shell." If the reader fails to understand the writing, then we (the writer and her language) have failed to do our job, which is to engage, entertain, or provoke the reader in some way. This assumes that the reader is interested in these ideas to begin with, and motivated enough to read the text. Not all writing, of course, is meant for all readers. Not all seed falls on fertile ground.

Storytelling is a necessary part of the human condition. We must tell stories. It is what makes us who we are. Linguists and neurologists strongly suspect that the act of learning language physically shapes the organization of our brains. Without language, we are incapable of the full range of human interaction and reasoning. By telling stories to our children, we give them language, and so a passport into the condition of human mortality. But also, a window onto the immortal, for stories will outlive all of us.

I have chosen (or have been chosen by) a specific set of ideas on which to concentrate my writing, and will turn all of my creative efforts towards conveying these ideas in the most accessible and memorable ways possible. I want these ideas to go out and re-form and repeat and re-create themselves in as many ways as possible. Their source might be forgotten, or misremembered. That is all right with me, because I think the ideas are more important than I am as an individual writer.

I want my writing to insinuate itself into the subconscious of the people of the Southwest, so that we might remember who we were and who we will be, since so little time is spent in the present. I feel as strongly about this as any fanatic. This is my job.

Kathleen Alcalá
January 19, 1999

Reading the Signs

I

In an anthology called *Reinventing the Enemy's Language*,[1] Inéz Hernández Avila writes about the *abrecamino*, a figure in traditional Aztec dance. This person is, literally, the one who opens the way. Sometimes, this person carries a broom, to sweep aside the evil. Always, this person is a woman.

At the beginning of this century, women writers of color find ourselves acting as abrecaminos, the ones who lead the way, opening a path into new frontiers for traditional signs and symbols. Our definition of literacy changes almost daily, so I am going to start by taking you a roundabout way, opening a path first through the elements of communication, then into a definition of literacy, and finally, into a discussion of its politics.

II

As a definition of literacy, I will offer this: to be literate is to know how to read the signs. That's why we have people talking about computer literacy. It's not really about reading the signs, it's about where to find them. What used to be in the newspaper is now on-line. What used to be on the wall in the alley is now on-line. We must teach people how to access the signs and symbols, but the signs themselves change very slowly, some of them not at all.

An ideal exercise in literacy for me would be this: a young man reads one of my stories in a high school literature class. He goes on-line to order one of my books, and sees that it is also available on tape. What's more, it is available on tape in Spanish, so he orders a copy for his grandmother, who has cataracts and no longer reads. By listening to this tape, the grandmother would complete the circle of my work, since the first stories I heard were from my aunts, and were told in Spanish. The stories remind the grandmother of stories she knows, and she tells them to her grandson, who posts one or two on his Web site.

Ethnobotanist Gary Nabhan would say that to know the landscape is a form of literacy. He is a writer who spends weeks at a time looking for indigenous gardens, then interviews the (primarily) women who cultivate them.[2] Embedded in the old language is often a description of the uses and properties of a plant. And in indigenous languages often lie great nuance and meaning for the natural elements, how we have, in the past, lived with the earth.

"I am compelled to continue in my family's legacy, to demonstrate an obdurate sensitivity to the natural world," says Warm Spring/Wasco Navajo poet Elizabeth Woody. "This sense of place is an instruction that upholds an honorable way of life. I am active in my art, by giving story, by observing and listening. . . . My parents, aunties, and uncles have reinforced this, especially the need to nurture the land through love."[3]

To be separated from one's indigenous culture, I would argue, is a form of illiteracy. When the early Franciscan priests went to New Mexico in order to establish missions, according to Ramón A. Gutiérrez in *When Jesus Came, the Corn Mothers Went Away*,[4] they regularly took children away from their Indian parents and raised them as slaves. They had no language, other than the language of servitude. They had no culture outside of the religious training offered by the priests. They were called *genízaros*, detribalized Indians, and were outcasts even from their own pueblos. This is a deliberately imposed form of illiteracy, one which we must fight even today.

III

When do we value literacy? When it is used to perpetuate a culture? When it is used to train children to get along in the predominant society? When it is used for profit?

To be literate is to know how to read the signs.

My goal for my son, who is eleven, is to teach him how to gather the necessary information and make an independent judgment. In a time when we are inundated with information, screening out the irrelevant is as crucial as gathering the essential. What's more, at an earlier and earlier age, children must learn skepticism. We cannot control their sources of information. But we can teach them to consider the source, and consider the motives of the source in disseminating the information. I mean, of course, advertising, but I think a healthy amount of skepticism can be brought to the educational and governmental systems within which we live as well. Besides, increasingly, it is difficult to separate advertising from content. If you watch a television commercial without the sound, what are they selling? Tight jeans? Trucks? Beer? Or political viewpoint?

I expect my son to be literate enough to run this gamut of information, infotainment, and spin while keeping his own sense of heritage, artistry, and individuality intact. To be able to produce information, and convey it to the appropriate audience, is as crucial a skill as being able to take in and process information. I think that too much emphasis is placed on students as passive receivers of information, on receiving and regurgitating information. The recent emphasis on test scores, will, I'm afraid, make that even more the case.

But maybe a literate population is too much of a threat. Leslie Marmon Silko writes in her collection of essays, *Yellow Woman and the Beauty of the Spirit,*[5] about "The Indian with a Camera." Silko grew up at Laguna Pueblo, and tourists have been pointing cameras at her all of her life, in one case, taking Leslie, who is mixed blood, out of a photo because she didn't look Indian enough. As an adult, Silko, who wrote novels such as *Ceremony,*[6] *Almanac of the Dead,*[7] and most recently, *Gardens in the Dunes,*[8] is also a photographer. She said that this makes the tourists really uncomfortable. Why? Because she, as an artist, is turning her gaze on them. Indians are supposed to be the passive receivers of *their* gaze. The implications of an Indian turning her gaze, her sensibilities, on them, capturing their images, is a subversion, a reversal of the given order.

That unspoken contract, that we will receive information, but not produce it or interpret it, is often applied to the rest of us as well. Writers of color can write about our own people, but very few have been taken seriously as commentators on society in general, or hold the tangential but very necessary roles of agents, editors, or publishers. These are all aspects of literacy, because these people control what you and your children will see in the bookstores next year.

Of course, the recent legislation towards English Only laws in California and elsewhere are part of this unspoken contract, but only the most recent manifestation of it. My father, who was the first Mexican hired to teach by the Orange County School District in California, lost his job when he refused to sign a Loyalty Oath. He couldn't sign, he said, because he wasn't a U.S. citizen. They then made it a requirement that he become a citizen to keep the job, but he couldn't gain his citizenship because he was a pacifist. This was during World War II. So instead, the INS tried to deport him. The effort was dropped after the war ended, but they succeeded in keeping him out of a public classroom. In the meantime, he applied for and was granted American citizenship, and later went on to teach in another district for many years. But those are just a couple of examples of what I'm calling the Unspoken Contract, that we will learn to be literate, but only half-way, in that we will not hold positions of interpreting the world at large for others.

So literacy, as many teachers have said, is a tool for survival. But it is much more than that. It is a way to manifest our place in the world. It is, for all the reasons I just talked about, a political act. If writers act as abrecaminos, the path openers, it's assumed that someone will follow, will take that path. The circle of literacy is only complete when someone reads the story, hears the song, and is able to respond in kind with new stories and new songs, whatever form they may take. As storyteller Vi Hilbert says, if you heard and understand this, you will say, Haboo.

For the series
"The Politics of Literacy at the Turn of the Century"
North Seattle Community College
February 2, 2002

The Madonna in Cyberspace

We have been asked to talk about why we are artists; why we do what we do, so I thought I would start with a little bit about what, exactly, a writer does.

Collectors

Writers collect things. We read magazines, we ride buses and eavesdrop on other people's conversations, we stop and read posters on telephone poles, we examine soup cans and old clothing stores and babies and pets and sewer covers and weather reports. We delve into ancient history, old gossip, rumors, hints of rumors, maps, brochures, irrelevant details, bad advice, good omens, lucky stars, and things that are nobody's business.

In short, we are called to be witnesses. Things may happen, but unless someone takes note of it, it might not matter.

C. Vann Woodward, a noted Southern historian, wrote in a paper titled "American Attitudes Toward History," that "the past is alterable to conform with present convenience, with party line, with mass prejudice, or with the ambitions of powerful popular leaders." So it makes a difference who acts as a witness. Woodward's writings were instrumental in overturning segregation laws in the fifties because he documented in *The Strange Career of Jim Crow*[1] that segregation in the South dated only to the 1880s. This countered arguments that a centuries-old way of life would be destroyed.

Connectors

The next thing that we do is link events together. Things may happen, but if they're not going to happen again, does it matter? We document cause and effect. If the roof collapses, the television will get wet. If the coffee is cold, the clients will be grumpy. If Sylvia receives roses, the mail will be delivered on time.

There's a wonderful story by Jorge Luis Borges, called "The Babylon Lottery,"[2] in which the people of a mythical kingdom take part in an elaborate game of chance where the rules keep changing. They engage in activities that seem increasingly random, such as dropping a bag of jewels into the river at midnight, yet it is imperative that they keep participating.

Sounds like life. We seek links between the different things that happen to us in order to make sense of life. We also seek any indication that we have some control over our destinies. In writing, this is called the narrative thread. This happened, then this, and this, and as a result, these other things happened. Sylvia received roses, and the mail was on time. Knowing in time that the roof was weak, Ted fixed it, and the television did not get wet. The coffee did not grow cold while Teresa shopped for a new television, and the clients were not grumpy.

Providing the narrative thread to life is one of the oldest functions in culture. People need storytellers. They make sense out of life. Instead of being an abstract concept, a road without an end, life becomes something that we can touch, hear, feel, taste, see. Chekhov gave us the Lady with the Dog,[3] James Joyce gave us Leopold Bloom,[4] Sandra Cisneros[5] gave us Woman Hollering Creek, and by creating the specifics of a life, they give us a *sense*, they make sense of, life.

Scribes for the Collective Culture

Some images are more effective than others, depending on your background and culture. Skagit storyteller Vi Hilbert tells me that the teller changes the story each time, depending on the setting and the audience.[6] There is always an optimum way to tell the story, and it's always different. Writers, as a rule, don't have that flexibility, but our best stories, those that are most effective, come from a place close to our hearts, and deeply imbedded in our cultures.

Every person seeks her own face in art, in movies, in literature; we look for people like ourselves so that we can see how alike, or how different, that image is from the one that we carry inside. We seek affirmation in those images, which is why so much time and money are spent on surveys about how many minorities appear on prime-time television. Television has become the mirror of our culture, and if we are not in it, we feel that we must not exist.

Artists do the same thing: we project ourselves into our work, and even if our faces are not overtly visible, as in Frida Kahlo's paintings, you certainly see our concerns and our worries and the objects that we consider beautiful and graceful and desirable. That's why it's so important that people of color not only be some of the actors on television and teachers in the schools where we study, but the writers, producers, editors, buyers, sales help, accountants, and owners where we do business. We look for our reflections everywhere, and writers and artists help to fill that need.

What is it we really seek? We seek the truth, about the world, and about ourselves. Not facts, but a true thing, an artifact that we all know but that has been obscured, and of which the story reminds us. They resonate with us, they ring like a bell when we see or hear them. These artifacts are called universal symbols, and art that endures draws on these universal symbols. These are symbols that cross cultural, sexual, racial, and age lines, symbols that, as nature writer Barry Lopez put it, remind us of things that we have forgotten.[7] We are all born knowing these things, but we must be reminded again and again by the artists and storytellers in our midst.

There is a reason why the garden, as a symbol, is used over and over—water and light, desert and sea, running away and coming home again. The repetition of names is important in many cultures—the aboriginal people of Australia, the roll call cane of the Iroquois nation, the Israelites in the desert. We recite the names of our ancestors in order to create a bond with the past, and to invoke their collective power. In the same way, we depict nature in paintings and in stories in order to invoke its spirits, to create a bond of both power and dependence between people and the landscape around us.

Messengers

In a way, artists are messengers between worlds, bringing ideas and symbols from one to the other. When I've actually wanted to make money, as opposed to writing great literature, this is what I've done for a living. I've had many job titles, but I've usually worked as a writer, and as a translator between cultures — turning broadcasting jargon into something people in rural Colorado would understand, trying to describe the spiritual needs of Native Americans to the Catholic archdiocese, writing grants on behalf of people who work with their hands, not with their mouths.

Artists are not merely the frosting on the cake of civilization, a frill that serves no real purpose. Remember, we work with symbols, and another word for symbols is *icons*, which brings us to the twenty-first century. Most of us correspond with people through e-mail. We already work with people as symbols, free-floating in a cyberspace where the virtual replaces the real. We might be free of the old ways of communicating, but we are not free of the old symbols, because, in the end, that's all we have.

Italo Calvino, in *The Uses of Literature*, said that "the more technological our houses, the more their walls ooze ghosts."[8] What does that mean? It means that the more abstract our dealings with each other, the more mysteries are created. The more mysteries, the more questions, and that's where the storyteller steps in. We invoke old symbols to answer new questions. The next generation will write new stories that link the new world to the old symbols. And this is how we pass things on. This is how the circle, another universal symbol, is completed, by linking the old with the new, the past with the present, the virtual with the real. The madonna, the lynx, the jaguar, the swan, all will stand as guardians to new gateways, new gardens, new jungles, and will still serve as messengers from one world to the next.

No matter what the venue, we can be witnesses to our own existence. "If we do not define ourselves for ourselves," said Audre Lorde, "we will be defined by others — for their use and our detriment."[9] Each generation must look around with a critical eye and ask, "Is this who I am? How will we be portrayed to future generations?" In cases where history has been misremembered or forgotten altogether, we must be brave and resourceful enough to restore it. This is not always easy, especially if it goes against the grain of popular thought.

That's what we do as artists: we collect, we connect, we serve as scribes for the collective culture, and as messengers between worlds. Most important, we bring these symbols to the public. This is our gift, our *regalo*, our ofrenda. But it's up to the reader, the viewer, the listener, to bring out the power of these stories, to call out their names, and give them a place in the world.

Presented at North Seattle Community College
January 14, 2000

Against All Odds

A couple of years ago I finished a book of short stories. The last story in the collection is called "La Esmeralda,"[1] and as I wrote it, I could feel something different emerging. It had a different rhythm to it, and by the time I finished, I realized that these characters were not finished with me. I had to write a novel. The story is set in the late 1800s in northeastern Mexico, in the Chihuahuan Desert and the city of Saltillo. I realized that the time and place called for a lot more information than I had, or could invent, so I started doing some research.

Wandering through the stacks at the University of Washington one day, I came across a book called *Against All Odds: The Feminist Movement in Mexico to 1940*.[2] I thought, "Oh, that might be interesting," so I looked at it, then checked it out, then read it through and went around ranting about it for several weeks.

This is one of those books that was as much an odyssey to write as it was about a chapter in history. Anna Macías, who is now a retired professor in the Midwest, spent countless hours poring through records in Mexico City to retrieve this information. When she first approached the subject, she was told by many Mexicans, "There has never been a feminist movement in Mexico." It turned out that the records of several *congresos* of women, national congresses, had been considered so insignificant that they had never been catalogued and shelved. They were still in boxes in the basement of the National Archives until she insisted on gaining access to them. There had been a strong feminist movement in the Yucatán from 1916 to 1923, and five feminist congresses, all organized by women, were held in Mexico in the 1920s and 1930s. Mexican women almost achieved the vote in 1939, yet very little had been written about it. Macías found that a significant feminist movement, involving thousands of women of every social class and whose origins go back to the seventeenth century, had developed from approximately 1890 to 1940.

Probably the first official feminist in Mexican history was Sor Juana Inéz de la Cruz, who lived from 1648 to 1695. During her lifetime, she was honored as the tenth Muse of Mexico, and known through the Americas and Europe for her wit and intelligence. She argued against a sexual double standard in her famous poem, *Hombres necios (Foolish Men)*:

> Which has the greater sin when burned
> By the same lawless fever:
> She who is amorously deceived,
> Or he, the sly deceiver?
> Or which deserves the sterner blame,
> Though each will be a sinner:
> She who becomes a whore for pay,
> Or he who pays to win her?[3]

Sor Juana argued for equality in education, but did not trust men to act as teachers. She suggested that a group of self-educated women should teach young females, instructing them not only in elementary subjects, but in literature, history, science, and theology as well.

By 1810, there were a few educational institutions for women, and by 1824, with the establishment of a republican form of government, more government officials stressed the need to end elitist education and to replace it with fundamental education for all. A good example of a plan was the 1826 "Project of a Decree Concerning Public Education in the Free State of Jalisco," in which the authors hoped that "the happy day will come in which this amiable sex, schooled in the august temple of the sciences, shall produce the remarkable spectacle of mesdames de Staels amongst us."[4] Their plan was to hire *preceptoras*, or women teachers, selected and paid by the municipality at a decent rate. However, very little was accomplished between 1824 and 1855. The political turmoil, aggravated by losing over half the territory of Mexico to the United States, distracted Mexico from the task of nation building. In fact, educational opportunities for all Mexicans probably regressed to that of about the early 1700s.

Benito Juárez, in outlining his program to the Mexican Congress on January 20, 1861, was the first president in Mexican history to state that "the education of women will also be attended to, giving it the importance it deserves because of the influence women exercise over society."[5]

But the long-promised secondary school for girls did not open its doors until 1869, followed in the next five years by similar schools around the country. The school in Mexico City was no sooner established than its female director requested that faculties in medicine, pharmacy, and agriculture be set up within that institution. But as social historian Luis González y González laconically put it, "*La idea no prosperó.*"[6] Most of its graduates became schoolteachers.

In addition, a vocational school for women was established in Mexico City, La Escuela de Artes y Oficios de Mujeres, which offered courses in embroidery, watchmaking, bookbinding, photography, tapestry-making, and telegraphy, and eight courses in basic scientific subjects. Most of the women who attended this school were from the working classes, according to Macías. By 1910, on the eve of the Mexican Revolution, there were more than four hundred women enrolled in the secondary school, and more than one thousand in the vocational school.

However, although the women who became schoolteachers were venerated and praised, and paid all of two pesos a day for their work, society under Porfírio Díaz was unwilling to permit women to teach beyond the primary grades. Until 1889, the graduates were certified to teach primary and secondary school, but after that date the course of study was reduced from six to four years and its women graduates certified to teach only in primary schools.

There was also considerable resistance to women becoming licensed doctors. Women had access to obstetrical courses, since women had always delivered babies, but there was entrenched reluctance to giving women the same medical training as men. Matilda Montoya was the first woman who, spurred on by the need to support her widowed mother, was determined to break down this prejudice. Since the government could not afford to establish a separate medical school for women, Montoya was finally allowed to attend classes at the National School of Medicine with male students in 1880. Her example inspired Columba Rivera, who became the second woman doctor in Mexico. Resistance ceased when people realized that there was a real need for women doctors, especially to care for women who refused to see a male doctor. Both Montoya and Rivera specialized in women's diseases.

The first woman to receive a law degree, María Sandoval de Zarco, met even more resistance. She scandalized *"la gente decente,"* decent people, when she agreed to represent a male defendant in a criminal case. After that, she was obliged to practice civil law only, as Mexico's lawyers thought it highly inappropriate for a woman to practice criminal law.

By the end of the Porfirian era, according to Macías, thousands of middle-class women worked as schoolteachers, with almost another two thousand working for the government. Between 1888 and 1904, the first women were accepted, however reluctantly, in the schools of medicine, law, and commerce in Mexico City.

In that case, why was there a need for a feminist movement? Many gains were made in the late 1800s and early 1900s, but there was another side to that era of economic progress, in which the railroads and telegraph systems were built, old mines reopened, textile and other industries established, and agricultural exports increased. While more middle-class women were studying and working than ever before, the number of poorer women who became domestic servants or prostitutes increased considerably from 1877 to 1910, according to Macías. In 1895, with a population of 12.7 million, Mexico had more than 275,000 domestic servants, most of them women, and most of them in virtual slavery. In 1907, with only one-fifth the population of Paris, Mexico City had twice as many *registered* prostitutes, and Paris was supposedly the Sin City of the West. About 30 percent of Mexican mothers were single parents. In addition, about 80 percent of the adult population lived in *amasiato*, or free union, in a society where illegitimate children had no legal rights to inheritance and could not investigate their paternity. This was due in part to the fees required by the Catholic Church to marry within the Church, the only legally sanctioned marriage in Mexico at that time. Most couples could not afford the fees.

Middle- and upper-class women had their own problems. The Civil Code of 1884 gave adult, single women almost the same rights as adult males, but a married woman became *"imbecilitas sexas —* an imbecile by reason of her sex."[7]

Feminist Hermila Galindo summed up the legal discrimination in the 1884 code:

> The wife has no rights whatsoever in the home. She is excluded from participating in any public matter and lacks legal personality to draw up any contract. She cannot dispose of her personal property, or even administer it, and she is legally disqualified to defend herself against her husband's mismanagement of her estate, even when he uses her funds for ends that are most ignoble and most offensive to her sensibilities. A wife lacks all authority over her children, and she has no right to intervene in their education. . . . She must, as a widow, consult persons designated by her husband before his death, otherwise she can lose her rights to her children.[8]

Why a woman should have her legal personality erased upon marriage was a mystery to the few lawyers who favored the legal emancipation of women; presumably the legislators thought that absolute power by the husband over his wife and children would make for domestic happiness.

In 1904, Dr. Columba Rivera, María Sandoval de Zarco, and a teacher, Dolores Correa Zapata, founded a feminist monthly, *La Mujer Mexicana*, which was owned and edited exclusively by women, and continuously published until 1908. Women began to speak out on social and economic problems. They called for more trained women to take part in Mexico's progress, and formed the "Sociedad Protector de la Mujer," one of the earliest feminist societies in Mexico, intended to help working-class women. Their first action was to establish a school and factory for embroiderers and hatters, to train unemployed women while paying them a just wage.

Nobody got too excited about this. These actions did not threaten male prerogatives, but now we return to Sor Juana's little poem. The next demand was for a single sexual standard. In November 1904, the editors of *La Mujer Mexicana* reprinted an article by the Spanish writer Concepción Gimeno de Flaquer that objected to the fact that, in Spanish and Latin American culture, polygamy was more general than monogamy, was tolerated by the church, and, even worse, given legal sanction in the Civil Code of 1884. When feminists protested against the inequity, critics insisted that they were advocating sexual license for women. Feminists countered that elevating the moral level of both men and women was the issue at stake.

This started getting reactions. The minister of public education, Justo Sierra, said, very politely, "I do not want to see you pursue your feminism to the extreme of wishing to convert yourselves into men; that is not what we desire; for then, all of life's enchantment would be lost. No; let men fight over political questions, let them form laws; you ought to fight the good fight, that of feeling, and form souls, which is better than forming laws."[9]

Less politely, an anonymous writer published an article in *El Monitor Republicano* stating that there were only five kinds of women, all bad and all guaranteed to be vexatious to their husbands:

"lacrimosas, dinerosas, artifisacias, santacias, o talentacias." The first are whiners and crybabies, the second spendthrifts, the third think only of appearance, and the fourth are forever praying and attending mass. The fifth, the "talentacias," are worst of all. They eat little, pay no attention to their appearance, constantly bemoan the ignorance of the masses, and consider themselves unfortunate because one lifetime is not enough to read even a millionth part of what has been written. These *literatas* cannot even dress or undress themselves without the help of maids.[10]

In a less humorous vein, an extremely conservative Yucatecan writer named Ignacio Gamboa wrote in 1904 in his book *La mujer moderna*, that feminism represented the suicide of the race. Feminists, he maintained, were against reproduction. He insisted that "los divorcios, las asociaciones femeniles contra el matrimonio, el vicio lesbico, que por una inmensa descracia toma gigantescas proporciones en los grandes centros de la poblacion . . ." — divorce, feminine assocations against matrimony, and the vice of lesbianism, which, by an immense misfortune assumes gigantic proportions in the larger cities — all resulted from the women's movement.[11]

Felix Palavacini, a writer and educator who championed women's rights at the Querétaro Constitutional Convention in 1916, had earlier said that an intellectual woman would produce physically weak or degenerate children. He quoted Herbert Spencer, who claimed that mental effort overtaxed women's brains resulting in "a serious reaction on the physique" of women and a "diminution of reproductive power."[12]

The feminist movement was continued by women educators. But I wanted to draw your attention to some of the women who were the first, against all odds, in their fields: Doctor Matilda Montoya, Dr. Columba Rivera, and lawyer María Sandoval de Zarco, who with Dolores Correa Zapata founded the feminist monthly *La Mujer Mexicana*[13]; feminist Hermila Galindo de Topete who was the private secretary of President Carranza, and later published her own journal, *La Mujer Moderna*, from 1917 to 1919[14]; and María Ríos Cárdenas, who founded the feminist journal *Mujer* in 1926.[15]

Mexican women did not begin to gain the right to vote until 1946, and did not vote in a presidential election until 1958.[16] Nevertheless, the pioneering work of these women deserves some attention.

Today, in the United States, we deal with a different set of statistics. Two-thirds of mothers in the United States work outside the home. One fourth of the children in this country live with only one parent, usually the mother. Twenty three million children require daycare[17] in a country with no national policy on daycare, and in which the President vetoed a family leave bill. And the Clarence Thomas hearings, in which Anita Hill represented all of us to a group of men who just didn't get it.

More families have fallen into poverty in the last few years. And yet, against these odds, we all know women who have succeeded.

Sandra Madrid, Assistant Dean of the Law School at the University of Washington; Angela Ginorio, PhD in psychology and Director of the Women's Information Center at the University of Washington; Virginia Apodaca, founder of MANA Northwest and later a top federal administrator in San Francisco; Cleo Molina at North Seattle Community College, State Representative Margarita Prentice; the Cavazo family; and of course, Hermelinda González, who left farmwork, got an education, and devoted her life to helping Central American refugees before succumbing to cancer at an early age.

Each of these women has a story. Each beat incredible odds to get where she is today. They, too, have given a helping hand to other women on the way up. That's what they have in common with the women of their grandmothers' and great-grandmothers' generations. They didn't stop worrying about equal rights and equal access when they made personal gains. They turned around and said, 'There's room for you, too.'

In the fall of 1975, I was in my last year of college. I was lucky. I got partial scholarships to Stanford and was able to make up the difference by working about twenty hours a week while attending classes full-time. I was very determined. But by my senior year, I was exhausted. I added up my pennies, and felt as though I just couldn't take on any more work. I figured out how much I needed and was crushed. It was more money than I could ask for from anyone, so I finally went to the bank. I was raised to think that loans were bad, that it was a compromise to put myself in debt, but I finally gave in. I was practically in tears when I talked to the loan officer, and I did cry when the loan was approved the next day. I had asked for five hundred dollars. That doesn't seem like much now, but it was what stood between me and my degree. I graduated a quarter early to take a job, and paid off that loan in 1978.

So what doesn't seem like much to you now, could mean a lot to someone else. We each know what we went through, but we can only guess at the odds facing young women today. But from among them will come the next century's Sor Juana or Matilda Montoya or Hermila Galindo or Elena Poniatowska or Margarita Prentice or Hermelinda Gonzalez. We are here speculating on futures, gambling that they will make it, against the odds, but with our faith and support bearing them up on wings of success.

Hispanic Women's Network
Olympia, Washington
September 26, 1992

Introduction to

Fantasmas: Supernatural Stories by Mexican American Writers

When I saw the announcement for *Fantasmas*,[1] my first thought was "Why haven't *I* been asked to contribute to this? After all, *my* work has been reviewed in *The New York Review of Science Fiction*. How fantastic is that?" But those were my secret thoughts. And secret thoughts are what these stories are all about.

Soon enough, Rob Johnson found me and soothed my ego by asking me to write this introduction, for which I am delighted.

Fantasmas are a particular kind of writing which is very popular in Mexico. My guess is that it is popular all over the world, as it serves as a bridge between traditional storytelling and pulp fiction, incorporating elements of both. Alberto Manguel has collected two volumes worth of fantastic literature in *Black Water and Black Water 2*.[2] In some cases, the stories take the reader right over the line to horror, the worst thing you can imagine fulfilled. In others, the fantastic elements are merely implied, and if the reader tried to pinpoint the specific elements that made the story fantastic, it would be impossible to do. Rather, the fantastic element lies in "the overall effect" that Edgar Allan Poe tried to infuse into each of his stories.

In Latin America, there hasn't necessarily been a clear line between fantastic literature and literary fiction. This has allowed writers like Jorge Luis Borges, Gabriel García Márquez and Clarice Lispector to be noticed by upstanding and respectable critics of modern culture, and has led to the eventual translation of their work, as well as that of many others. They now form a canon of work against which all the rest of us must be compared, although, in many cases, we have little in common with them other than the Spanish language.

As far as I know, this is the first collection of fantastic literature specifically by Mexican Americans, and it contains elements that make these stories unlike any others. These stories are not, for example, mostly inspired by American and European written forms, as are the "standard" published Latin American *cuentos de fantasma*. If forced to generalize about specific elements that make the border stories chosen for this collection unique, I would include the following: (1) basis in oral tradition, (2) influence of folk religions, (3) use of vernacular forms, (4) influence of life and culture from the U.S. side of the border.

Unfortunately, some of these elements will be seen by critics as reinforcing certain stereotypes in Mexican-American literature. For example, an early manuscript reader of this book commented, "Serious Mexican-American short story writers have been struggling their entire careers to create work that does not fit the stereotype that 'all Mex. American lit is about curanderos, la llorona, tortillas, and family superstitions.' " I think this response says more about the reviewer than the book itself, but it gives us a chance to talk about some very interesting things. My parents' generation had to spend a great deal of time convincing people that Mexicans were capable of holding jobs outside the level of farm worker or menial labor, and part of this was showing an "advanced" view of the world. In the forties and fifties, this meant being very patriotic, giving your children "American" (British) names and not appearing to be too superstitious or backwards. In other words, it was a class thing, and being Mexican was equated with being lower class. Of course it still is, but the ability of the writers in this collection to look at these symbols with irony, with affection, and with an eye towards their mythological value shows a generational shift in aesthetic viewpoint, from encouraging the production of literature depicting Mexican-Americans in a socially acceptable light (the society being white), to literature being written to express all that our culture has to offer, and not really caring what others think of us as a result.

My own relationship to this type of story spans several generations. In my library is a book called *Relatos misterio y realismo*,[3] published in Mexico in 1947 and written by José García Rodríguez. Each of his stories tells of ordinary people who go about their business and have an encounter, or near encounter, with the fantastic. In almost every case, the protagonist is saved from disaster by behaving in a decent or just manner. These are tales with morals—the weak are prey to the devil. But there is also an element of coincidence—

had he taken this road rather than that — in the stories, as exemplified by "Michele's Miracle" by Kelly Jácquez.[4] What, really, is fate, and what control do we have over it?

While written in a manner that was probably modern for their time, the roots of García Rodríguez' stories in the folk tales of Mexico are evident. Universally, folk tales have been used to educate and entertain, to show acceptable behavior by example, and perpetuate the ways of a particular culture. In other words, these are didactic tales, and have their roots, in turn, in mythology.

This is the way that we explain the world to ourselves and each other. It is how we teach our young to survive.

García Rodríguez was a relative of mine, so the stories he was hearing and retelling are not too different from the folk history of my immediate family. As my sister pointed out to a group of Ladies Who Lunch in Fargo, North Dakota, while they were discussing one of my more cryptic stories, what is *not* told is often as important as what *is* told. The imagination must be given free rein for these stories to work, and that is what gives them their universality and staying power. Unlike a television series that is forgotten the next season (except for *Star Trek*,[5] of course, which a friend who is a professor of comparative literature insists is all taken from *The Odyssey*), cuentos of this nature can be retold again and again without losing their punch.

Rob Johnson generated some of these stories by asking his students to take folk tales and retell them in a modern setting. While the stories still retain their timelessness, this introduced two elements that I really enjoy: the urban legend and modern dialect. Growing up in San Bernardino, we had the urban legend of The White Albino. The name for this person is redundant, one of the great things about this story. He escaped from prison, where he was serving time for murder. He lived in the San Bernardino Mountains, where he saved a young couple from certain death in a snowstorm. Or murdered them, or almost murdered them and they drove away with the hook that he used instead of a hand in the handle of the car . . .

Wait a minute, you say. This sounds familiar. Of course. It's an urban legend, with all of the elements of fear and mystery *of that particular place* introduced — incarceration, the mountains, being caught out late with your boyfriend, and extra-white people. The ambiguous nature of The White Albino is what makes the story linger in the mind. Did he mean them harm, or was he trying to help them? Can we judge people by their looks? Their color? Their past?

The power of place—a crucial element of the literature of the west and southwest—is evident in all of the stories in *Fantasmas*. By using local, modern dialect, these stories are tied to landscape and culture in a way that draws on the rich imagery of our everyday lives. Like the house with the blinds always drawn, or the cross and flowers by the roadside, each feature of our landscape embodies a story. By their language, you can see these girls with their big hair and painted nails, these guys in their skinny jeans, and know that, yes, things like this happen to regular people. People like you, or at least what you used to be like when you were young and skinny. Reading these stories will make you recall half a dozen more, and that's the point of literature—to tell and retell the stories that make us human, to dip into the common well of our consciousness and bring up a detail that links us to each other.

One aspect of fantastic literature that must be noted is its political content. Starting with Alejandro Carpentier in Cuba, who probably first used the term "magic realism"[6] to describe literature, such fiction has been used as a vehicle for conveying political and social truths that could be fatal if presented more baldly. In spite of their careful eloquence, many of its practitioners have lived out their lives in exile as a result of their work. This is the extraordinary power of the written word: that it can make dictators, surrounded by militia, tremble in their boots. In *Fantasmas*, the dictators have been transformed into packing shed bosses, abusive husbands, and the turbulent desires of the heart. As Chilean writer Ariel Dorfman said, "When people who have nothing demand everything, that's real magic."[7]

Apparently, when we talk about magic, we talk about love. As Torie Olson writes in "Tear Out My Heart," "There is a milagro for every body part, but only the hearts come in super size. It appears that, more than anything else, people are sick at heart."[8] These stories are in large part about desire—what we really want, and what we will do to get it. In many cases, extreme sexuality, violence and revenge are linked to supernatural powers, some incarnation of the devil, as in "Lillith's Dance" by Gary G. Hernández.[9] These stories talk about our hidden impulses, and throughout history, I'm sure, these tales have been used as an outlet for the parts of the subconscious over which we feel we have no control. The implication is that these devils are contained within each of us, and we must strive every day to contain them. In our particular blend of pragmatism and mysticism, the person in the story might ask the Devil if he takes Visa before beginning to bargain.

There are no gauzy angels in these modern interpretations, no apparitions of the Virgin Mary, or bleeding icons. Rather, we must be angels to one another, we must incarnate the good as well as the bad. As Stephanie Reyes points out in "Bad Debts and Vindictive Women,"[10] these tales, traditionally, are supposed to have a moral. After reading them, I thought about this and decided that, if there is a common moral to the stories in *Fantasmas*, it is this: If you love someone, don't forget to tell them. Because when it's your time, it's your time.

So light some candles, put on some te de canela (you don't have to drink it—smelling it is good enough) and let us tell you about women with burning lips, men with long knives, and why you should never put a frog between your legs. . . .

The Transforming Eye of Kathleen Alcalá

Rob Johnson

Three years ago I began researching a type of story written by Mexican and Mexican-American writers called *cuentos de fantasmas*, literally "phantom" or "ghost" stories, but what I would generally describe as supernatural stories. Before long I came across Kathleen Alcalá's *Mrs. Vargas and the Dead Naturalist* (1992), a story collection she introduces with the following thoughts: "These stories are about inner landscapes; they explore the invisible world behind the visible, and the characters who move in both worlds through the windows of dream and imagination." Her words captured the spirit of my anthology, and I was pleased and grateful when she agreed to write the "Introduction" to *Fantasmas* (Bilingual Press, 2001). Alcalá is obviously happy for her work to be known for its element of fantasy, a quality that distinguishes her fiction from the social realism of the . . . *and the Earth Did Not Devour Him*–school of Chicano literature. In a story by Lucrecia Guerrero in *Fantasmas*, for example, a character *is* devoured by the earth after being cursed by her mother, and that's the kind of occurrence that could also happen in an Alcalá story.

This does not mean that Alcalá ignores social reality in her story collection and three novels (the opposite is true); it simply means that there is more than meets the eye in her fictional world. In *Mrs. Vargas and the Dead Naturalist*, there are indeed fantastic stories of mermaids singing and magical cameras and birds of ill-omen. "The Transforming Eye" shows a young woman impossibly entering the trompe l'oeil backdrop in a photo shop:

> Impatient, I stepped back into the portrait area to see if the photographer was there. The lights were on, and the backdrop glowed enticingly. On the stone bench in the scene was a wooden

bowl full of deliciously red pomegranates. They looked so real that I couldn't restrain myself from reaching to pick one up. The leathery skin and prickly end felt as real to me as any fruit I had ever touched. I turned with the pomegranate in my hand and saw that I stood on the black and white tiles, the bright trees trailing their branches over my head. . . . I was inside the backdrop.

Unbelievable, yes, but this expert bit of *legerdemain* is grounded in the reality of the death of the narrator's grandmother in Mexico, and the tears that are cried in the fountain in the photographer's *faux* backdrop rob her of her grief in reality. Here and elsewhere in the collection, the hidden "moral" of the story is reminiscent of the subterranean meaning found in the early works of Nathaniel Hawthorne, another writer for whom the "middle ground" of romance was native territory. This comparison is not farfetched: The title story of Alcalá's collection, for example, is a subtle allegory of how science seeks to destroy the very object it observes, the theme of many of Hawthorne's tales, such as "Rappacinni's Daughter." In this respect, I have to wonder why Joyce Carol Oates ignored Alcalá in her anthology *American Gothic Tales* (1997), for Alcalá's works would have complemented the stories Oates did select by Hawthorne, Flannery O'Connor, Stephen Millhauser, and others. (There are no Mexican-American writers in Oates' "American" collection.)

.:~ .:~ .:~ .:~ .:~

In the three novels that have followed *Mrs. Vargas and the Dead Naturalist*, you can see Alcalá moving beyond (or perhaps deeper into) what Ursula K. LeGuin once called "Alcalá-land" and exploring a past that can make us see our present differently — and may be evocative as well of a yet unseen future. Alcalá is, in other words, a visionary writer, which puts her in the company most closely of Leslie Marmon Silko, whose revelatory novel *Almanac of the Dead* (1991) is based on Native-American prophecy. In her novels, Alcalá reveals the often hidden identity of the people of the Southwest and Northern Mexico, covering territory that no American writer before her has traveled.

.:~ .:~ .:~ .:~ .:~

Spirits of the Ordinary (1997) tells the story of one such hidden people. Julio Vargas Caraval, his wife Mariana, and their son Zacarías are the descendants of Jews who trace their history back to the late sixteenth century, when the governor of Saltillo, Luis Carvajál, was imprisoned for admitting he was a Jew. At his trial, he declared that "were it not for the Inquisition, there would be fewer Christians in this kingdom than he could count on the fingers of his hand." The book concludes with another account of religious persecution in the late nineteenth century, the slaughter of Indians at Casas Grandes by the Mexican military. In its dramatization of the role the spirit plays in peoples' lives, Alcalá's novel moves beyond typical "people's history." *Spirits of the Ordinary* is in fact a deeply religious novel, full of marvelous translations from Hebrew into Spanish and finally into English. Its history of Mexico's Jews and of the spiritual beliefs of the *indígenes* are, remarkably, brought together in their common prophecy of a "Fourth World."

∴ ∴ ∴ ∴ ∴

The excitement of reading the novel comes from the unexpected variety and richness of the cultures represented in nineteenth-century Mexico. Here, for example, is a beautifully full picture of turn-of-the-century Saltillo:

> Horacio put on his coat and hat and let himself out of the shop. The bell clanged behind him as he shut the door firmly. Already the streets were filling with people — cooks buying food for the day, firewood vendors, bankers, traveling businessmen. His grandsons would be in school, and their sisters helping their mothers with household chores. Early mass was over, and the black-shawled widows cast shadows in the early-morning sun.
>
> Horacio made his way to the narrower streets of the Arab quarter and turned in at a shop with the word "Babilonia" written in white script over the door. An unfortunate name, thought Horacio, in a Christian country. But then, Ahmed would be too stubborn to admit that, since it was the city of his birth.

We sense as we read the novel that this is a story that has been in front of us always, just ignored. Elsewhere, Alcalá has described her mission as a writer in this way: "I want my writing to insinuate itself into the subconscious of the people of the Southwest, so that we might remember who we were and who we will be." Even for those of us who live in the Southwest (such as myself) these books are literally eye-opening.

❖ ❖ ❖ ❖ ❖

Alcalá's second novel, *The Flower in the Skull* (1998) is connected to the first with overlapping characters and by its uncovering of another "hidden" people. The second novel feels different than the first, though, as it is written in an oral style that employs repetition (with variation) and a circular plot-line. *Flower* dramatizes the fate of three women who are descendants of the Opata Indians of Mexico and the United States, a people whose culture has nearly been erased by a succession of colonial powers. The character Rosa captures this mixture of races in her own search for identity:

> It made me wonder what it meant to be related to someone, to be part this or part that. I was part Irish, because of my father, and I was part Indian, because of my mother. But I felt more Mexican than either of them, like the Morenos. We all spoke Spanish and lived in the same part of town and went to school together with the other Mexicans. Sometimes the children called me india because of my mother, but not very much, because some of the Mexican children were much darker than I was, and were probably just as india as I was, if not more.

Throughout the book, Alcalá complicates any simple identity politics, questioning as she does, for example, the real difference between Mexican-Americans and Native-Americans, labels which are starting to make less and less sense. This aspect of her work has the potential to startle American audiences complacent in their acceptance of "multiculturalism" by literally transforming what we see when we view the people of the Southwest and the Border.

❖ ❖ ❖ ❖ ❖

As a visionary work, *The Flower in the Skull* succeeds, for me, by revealing its meaning through a series of richly symbolic, sometimes startling transformations and magic lantern-type effects. Here in

The Flower in the Skull is Alcalá's description of the lamp shop of Alma Prieta, a *curandera* who is consulted by Concha about the wisdom of marrying Rosa to the evangelical minister Gabriel:

> In its front window was a lit kerosene lamp glowing through a wide rawhide shade and illuminating a scene that never failed to draw me closer as I passed by. On it was painted a series of scenes of Indians and white pioneers. . . . [The Indians] had their heads shaved except for a small piece like a porcupine, and rode tall horses and lived in pointed houses with poles sticking out of the top. . . . The other side of the lampshade showed Anglos bundled up in many clothes in horse-drawn wagons. Even the wagons were covered up, as though wearing huge bonnets. In each scene, a few men rode ahead of the others on their horses. They appeared to be leading the way. But since all of them were heading in the same direction on the shade — to the left — the two parties would never encounter each other. It was the perfect solution to the West — the bravos leading the way, followed by the children, the women, and the dogs, then a little space followed by the men pioneers, followed by their families. As long as they continued to circle the lampshade, they would never run out of frontier. They would never run into each other and have to fight.

Such camera obscura moments fill Alcalá's work and stay with the reader afterwards. In the first novel, a barren desert becomes transformed for Zacarías into its ancient form as an ocean bed, and he momentarily views vast whales sounding the desert floor. Photographs are a key medium in Alcalá's questioning of appearance versus reality (as in the magical camera of "The Transforming Eye"). In *The Flower in the Skull*, Concha begins the book in first person, telling her story of her life with the Opata before they are uprooted. Later, we see her through her daughter Rosa's eyes, and finally in a photograph discovered eighty years later by a young researcher in Arizona named Shelly. This photograph of an Opata woman living in a culture but clearly not being of that culture becomes Shelly's most valued possession — and the writer's. She studies Concha in the curling picture, and imagination and dreams reveal the story that lay hidden in old photographs stored in shoe boxes, stories that are (mostly) lost. At the end of the book, Shelly embarks on a pilgrimage to Magdalena, and sitting disoriented and road-weary in a café, she is joined by a waitress taking her break. "Tell me your story," she says to Shelly.

$$\ast \quad \ast \quad \ast \quad \ast \quad \ast$$

Kathleen Alcalá is a storyteller I continue to listen to. I live in McAllen, Texas, eight miles from the Mexican border at Reynosa, three hours by car from Saltillo and other places in Northern Mexico Alcalá writes about. I read her work for a fundamental reason: she opens my eyes and shows me, literally, a new way of seeing who I am, the people I live among, and the place where I live. Her forthcoming novel, *Treasures in Heaven*, will complete her trilogy of works on nineteenth-century Mexico. This novel, too, deals with yet another "hidden" people in Mexico — the women who played a crucial role in the political events leading up to the 1910 Revolution. Estela and other characters from the first two novels are also characters in this third novel.

$$\ast \quad \ast \quad \ast \quad \ast \quad \ast$$

I recently e-mailed Kathleen Alcalá a list of questions/observations, asking her about some of the issues raised above, and also about her new novel *Treasures in Heaven*. My questions and her written responses follow:

RJ: In your "Introduction" to *Fantasmas*, you write that the stories are about the search for love. The first time I read that, I thought it an odd way to describe stories in a collection of supernatural literature. However, after reading all of your work, I see, for example, that you consistently describe love as the link between higher (supernatural) and lower (natural) realms. *Spirits of the Ordinary* begins with a quotation from *The Zohar*: "In love is found the secret of divine unity. / It is love that unites the higher / and the lower stages of existence, / that raises the lower to the level of the higher — / where all become fused into one." And in *The Flower in the Skull*, for me, one of the most insightful (and moving) moments occurs when Concha, near the end of her life, realizes that "she has spent her life yearning for a past that didn't really exist, and never had." What she has really missed is her mother's affection, which she yearned for and never received. She had thought that what she needed was to return to a place, but what she learns is that place is only holy, only sacred, because it is made so by love.

KA: Stories of the supernatural are stories of transformation, from one state to another. Love is the strongest transformational force that we know, and also the one most sought after on a daily, ordinary basis. These stories, for the most part, were not tales of alienation, which might have been expected if this were a collection of strictly horror stories, but of people searching for connections, usually to others. When our drive to connect, to transform ourselves from one state to another (unhappy to happy, unloved to loved, shackled to free) is so strong that it seems to exceed the limits of the physical world, then we may invoke the otherworldly on our own behalf. And sometimes there is a response, but not always in the ways that we expect.

I think that Concha's yearning for place is valid. There is a love of place that transcends the love of individuals. In a traditional culture, this love is expressed through ritual and stewardship of the land. These rituals tie people together in the course of their daily lives, so that we identify love of family and culture with place. Place, under these circumstances, is holy.

But Concha had also enshrined the memory of her mother as the anchor of her former life. The person on whom she had depended the most was also the person who abandoned her to her fate, but after years had passed, Concha could see that it could probably not have been prevented. Whether she knew it or not, Concha's mother, in the act of abandonment, probably saved Concha's life.

When Concha leaves her village, she is little more than a child, with an experience of the world limited to her village and family. In fact, traditional village life at that time was designed to reinforce a fear of the unknown, of the outsider. It was designed to keep people tied to place as a means of survival, of perpetuating the crops, the culture and the group.

After years in Tucson, although she is still very provincial, she encounters her long-lost brother Beto, who tells her stories of his survival of the tragedy that killed their mother, and of his subsequent travels in the world. Only then can Concha see that there are many stories, and that her story is only one of them. While this does not necessarily make her a happy person, I think that it does give her some closure on the past. Whether she knew it consciously or not, Concha probably understood that the past could not be re-created, in that she had never tried to visit or return to her village.

RJ: Critics often call you a "magical realist." Yet you came to the works of "magical realists" after you yourself arrived at a similar place in your own work. How did this occur? What led you to combine an interest in the physical and metaphysical world?

KA: Growing up, I heard family stories, and I read a lot. Since we were in church half the time, I used to sit there and read the Bible, which, like Shakespeare, encompasses most of the human condition. I also read a lot of everything else, and especially liked science fiction, perhaps because that approach to storytelling validated the Mexican POV of many possibilities. I don't know. In any case, I never made a distinction between realistic and magic realistic writing. The first book I read that probably fell into the accepted canon of magic realism was *One Hundred Years of Solitude*, by García Márquez, maybe in 1972 or '73. I remember I found a copy in Spanish later and sent it to my parents, because it was so like our family stories. I also made my husband read it before we married, so that he would understand what sort of a family he was getting into.

About the time I got serious about writing fiction, I came across an article on magic realism by Yvonne Yarbro-Bejarano, written as an introduction to a Seattle production of *Blood Wedding*, by Federico García Lorca. It included a reading list. That was the first time I had thought of this type of writing as a school, or approach. That was probably in 1984.

This is literature that talks about not just the transformation of the individual, but of society.

RJ: You have named Leslie Marmon Silko as an influence. What can you say about the importance of her work, and what can you say about the link between Mexican-Americans and the indigenous people of the Americas. I know where I live, it's clear that the Indians never left.

KA: While I was writing *The Flower in the Skull*, I was sometimes overwhelmed with the feeling that no one in contemporary culture would care what I was talking about, that I was addressing this book to the dead. During that time, I read *Almanac of the Dead*, and here were these ideas, these stories, this understanding of the relationship of the people of the Southwest to the land, and the immateriality of the political border to traditional cultures. It was not written to flatter or beguile. She did not pull any punches. It was written to show these connections between the seen and the unseen, the past and the future. By talking about the Yaqui, who live on both sides of the border, she highlighted another culture, like the Opata, who have claims that supersede current boundaries. It was a great relief to find her work.

RJ: You have written to me that you prefer the term "Border" literature to the nation-specific labels such as Mexican-American. Can you elaborate on this?

KA: These labels are always a drag. I am sometimes asked if I am Spanish, because it is considered impolite or insulting to ask if I am Mexican, especially by Anglo Americans in the Southwest. Mexican American feels like the next politest thing to ask. Because of the location along the Tex/Mex border, the vigor and somewhat transgressional nature of these stories, I think it would be appropriate to call them Chicano, but as you say, your students associate that term with old people like me. Border literature implies the ability to dip into both cultures and step back and forth across the border. This area was a place of cultural convergence long before the Spanish or Americans showed up. By its very nature, the Southwest has always encouraged the cross-pollination of cultures, so border literature appeals to me.

RJ: *Spirits of the Ordinary* is a deeply religious work influenced by Christianity and its many expressions (Catholic, Evangelical), Judaism, and the religious beliefs of the indigenous peoples of North America. Is there a single, overlapping cosmological story you are telling here? Or are you more interested in pointing out those curious intersections of world religions — for example, the idea of Four Worlds that is common to both Judaism and the indígenes of Casas Grandes. I can't remember where I read this, although I believe I have read it more than once, that in the nineteenth century in the United States there was a popular theory that the Native Americans were descendants of a lost tribe of Israel.

KA: It was a lot of trouble to figure out how these three world views could be worked into this novel, but I felt that it was necessary in order to tell this story completely. The influences are clearly visible, in retrospect, in the way the cities and towns of the SW have developed, especially in Northern Mexico. It's not an accident that the North is politically independent from central Mexico. It's not an accident that Pancho Villa was from the north, and Francisco Madero, the first president after Porfírio Díaz. Madero was a practicing spiritualist who wrote several books which he claimed were dictated to him by his dead brother.

Finding the quote from *The Zohar* was as great a relief to me as finding Leslie Silko's work. I carried that quote around with me for about two weeks. It is about finding the universal in the specific. Not only are each of us part of the whole, but a single act of kindness is an act of universal grace. A single act of cruelty is a falling away of a bit of the whole for which we are all striving. The belief of students of the Cabala that the very act of meditating on its words will hasten the coming of the Messiah, implies that we each have a part to play in knitting up the fabric of the universe. The indigenous impulse to accept foreign religions and incorporate them into existing practice is due to the fact that the indigenous, for some reason, seem to understand that this is merely a partial view of the whole. I would have to study for the rest of my life to really understand these ideas, but I tried to incorporate them into the actions and motivations of the characters in *Spirits of the Ordinary.*

RJ: Could you describe your research methods in Mexico? What libraries have been of greatest use to you? How are you received? As an outsider? As an insider?

KA: I was nervous about going to Mexico City — as a Chicana, I had encountered people from Mexico who consider us despicable, traitors or something, because our parents left, or the old class thing, that we were lower class. My Spanish is not great, so I translated my questions into Spanish, and had examples of what I was looking for. I also had names of people to call once I got there, who were very helpful in telling me where things were, who I should ask for.

I would go to an archive or library, and surrender my credentials — in my case, this turned out to be my driver's license. Then I asked for what I needed, and was told that it was missing, inaccessible due to construction, or somewhere else. Then I went to the next thing on my list. Eventually, the librarians would start to bring me things, and when the right document showed up, I would praise them highly, ask for more like that one. Basically, I just would not go away until I got what I wanted. I don't consider myself very aggressive, but by Mexican standards, I seem to have been. People were too polite to refuse me. I had expected to run out of resources after a few days and become a tourist, but it never happened. I was incredibly fortunate.

I used the Archivo Nacionál, which is downtown, the Hemeroteca at the Universidad de México, the archives of the PIEM — the women's studies program at the Colégio de México, and the archives of the Universidad Hebraica. I also went into as many bookstores as possible and just looked around. The best bookstore for my purposes was the Librería Madero.

Just as helpful were the people I met every day. As I said, I had a couple of names, and these people were very gracious, inviting me into their homes and giving me their perspective on arts and literature and politics in Mexico today. But I also talked to taxi drivers, vendors, people I met in Tepotzlán. It helped me understand how things work in Mexico, and especially that Mexico City is one of those Center of the Universe cities, like New York and Paris, where things are of lesser importance the farther they are from the Center. No one was rude to me, or condescending. I had a wonderful time, and hope to return regularly for the rest of my life.

RJ: Your novel, *Treasures in Heaven*, deals with the feminist movement in Mexico in the nineteenth century and its relation to the seeds of the 1910 Revolution. Do you see a similar rise in feminism among Mexican women today?

KA: When we use the term *feminism* in nineteenth-century Mexico, it means something entirely different from what Americans think of as feminism from the 1960s or '70s. Feminists in Mexico, at that time, were fighting for state-funded education for women. They were fighting for legitimate employment for women, fair wages and working conditions. Women had actually lost legal status in the mid-1800s under the rewriting of the constitution after independence from Spain, and women did not get the vote in Mexico until the 1950s.

I suppose the fight is not too different today, including the search for cheap labor by the United States, and the search for foreign capital by the government of Mexico. The upper-class women I met in Mexico City seemed very advanced in their ideas, but only two I met also held a position of power to match. Other women I met went about their own business, and seemed almost studiously uninterested in the greater world. This could simply be one way to cope with the overwhelming complexities of living in a city like Mexico.

I think that it still takes a very motivated—either by need or exceptional ability—woman to succeed in Mexico today. In a country where the minimum wage is the equivalent of three dollars a day, most working-class women are still too busy putting food on the table to organize. The teachers' union is very powerful, and it will probably be through some sort of labor movement, rather than strictly social or cultural, that real change will come about.

Interview on Web site of the *American Center for Artists*
www.americanartists.org
September 1999[1]

V
9/11

Words That Heal, Words That Bind

I recently received a note from Kris Molesworth, executive director of Northwest Bookfest, that I wanted to share with readers of *The Seattle Times*.

"Although our small staff spent a good deal of time after September 11th feeling as though our work was somewhat trivial," she wrote, "I now believe exactly the opposite. The need to celebrate the power of the written word, the intellectual freedoms we hold dear, and the ability of literature to transport us is stronger than ever."

My own experience during the past weeks has been similar. My emotions have ranged from utter disbelief to fear to realizing that I could not possibly comprehend what had happened, really happened, to the people of New York City, Washington, D.C., and Pennsylvania, much less the motivations of the people who caused it.

And yet, and yet . . . I began to receive e-mails from people as far away as Chile and Greece expressing sorrow and solidarity. I began to receive stories of friends who, like David Paul, stopped at a mosque near his home to affirm friendship with his neighbors. I received angry e-mails and placating e-mails and finally, poetry. People turned again and again to writing poetry, and seeking out poems by great writers speaking of different times and places. Their words were searing, but at the same time, cleared a path by which I could begin to approach our new place in the world.[1]

Ten days later, weary from lack of sleep, I almost skipped a reading sponsored by *The Raven Chronicles* at the Richard Hugo House, but I didn't. There, I found people from all backgrounds and walks of life who had converged to bring their responses to the small stage. One woman drove all the way from Yakima to read a short poem. Another read a remarkable essay as cogent as anything I had heard on the radio or read in the paper. I slept for the first full night after the event.

For this is the role of the writer. By telling stories, we weave a narrative thread that ties our experiences together. The aftermath of September 11th has been flooded with stories of heroic deeds, of mysteries, loss, and simple friendship. In other words, the full tapestry of the human experience. This is how we make sense of the world. Storytelling is the glue of civilization.

Northwest Bookfest, for the seventh year, offers a place to gather, to share ideas, to reflect on the events in our lives, and open ourselves to the stories and experiences of others. It is a sea of ideas. We write, and celebrate the written word, not to forget, but to remember. We hope that you will join us for a weekend of laughing, of crying, of listening, and reveling in the wonder of words and life.

The Seattle Times
October 18, 2001

The Stone House

Once there was a woman who lived in a stone house. It had a beautiful garden, and a view of the hills beyond. In the winter, the hills were green. In the summer they were brown, like young deer grazing. Sometimes, she could see people on the hill. As time passed, there were also houses. The house was warm in winter and cool in summer, and the woman came to inhabit it like an extension of herself.

One day, a man came to her house. As soon as she opened the door, she knew who he was. Although she had never met him before, she could see that he, too, belonged to the stone house. She could see it on his skin and in his eyes. She could see it in the yearning way that he looked beyond her to the interior of the stone house.

Sure enough, the man had grown up in the stone house, and had lived there before her. His family had built it. Now, the man lived beyond the hills that were green in the winter and brown in the summer. The woman invited the man in to see the house again, and as they went from room to room, he told her all about his family. She left him for a moment in the room he had slept in with his brothers when he was a boy, and he lay his hand on every surface — on the walls, the smooth material of the bedspread, and flat against the window pane — as though to remember it through his hands.

Afterwards, the man and woman kept in touch and he called her now and then, although he did not come to visit.

A few years later, the man was arrested and sent to prison. The woman did not know where he was, only that she had not heard from him. After he was released fifteen years later, he tried to call her, but she did not return his calls. A long time had passed, and many things had changed.

More years went by, and the woman's father, who had lived with her in the stone house, died. She tried to decide what to do with the house. She called up the man who had once lived there, and offered to sell him the house. But the people who ran her country said that he could not own the house, although he had once lived there. Then the woman offered to sell the house and give the man and his family the money from it, because she felt that it was rightfully theirs. But the man refused, saying that the money meant nothing to him, only the house.

Finally, the man who had once lived in the stone house had an idea. He asked the woman to start a school for children, a school that would include children who lived near the house, and children who lived beyond the green and brown hills where he now lived. She agreed, and the two of them have become friends again, by keeping the stone house as a place for her people, and his. The children visit the stone house every day, and learn songs, and learn about each other, because their common love for the stone house is stronger than the differences that once kept the owners apart. The woman is an Israeli, and the man a Palestinian. But the children, at least in the stone house, are only children.

Exhibition, 2002
Based on a feature story, by Sandy Tolan,
heard on NPR "Weekend Edition,"
September 8, 2001

Dear John

A Letter to a Friend Following 9/11

In the aftermath of 9/11, I received e-mails expressing a range of emotions, both reactionary and patient in trying to understand this tragedy. A writing acquaintance who had recently moved out of state sent out an e-mail that called for quick retaliation against the perceived enemy. After some thought, this is what I wrote[1]:

Dear John—

I was torn. I talked about this a little in a letter that was published in the October 18 *Seattle Times*. I don't believe that bombing people will solve anything. I see our administration having cold war responses in a world that has changed quite a bit in the last 25 years.

My son just turned 12 years old, and I see us at the brink of 10, 15 or more years of pouring all of our resources into creating more destruction at the expense of culture, literacy, and education not only in our country, but all over the world. Twenty thousand people who thought they were about to enter this country legally have been put off indefinitely. These are, in large part, the high-tech and skilled workers we desperately need. Thousands more laborers from Mexico and Central America are not coming, because the borders really have been closed. We have been plunged into an economic depression that had already been started by this administration, and will be exacerbated by the war mentality. We are merely reacting to extremists, rather than acting on behalf of a country, a people, who once had high ideals of freedom and democracy.

One person on NPR said, the greatest single cause of terrorism is poverty. We are not going to eradicate poverty by bombing people. Even if we carpet bomb every inch of Afghanistan, we are not going to catch bin Laden unless he is surrendered by people who see a better way. Are we showing them a better way? I don't think so. Do I have any global answers? No. All I can say is that we must live compassionately, consider the consequences of what we buy, what we eat, and spread knowledge, all knowledge, when given the opportunity. When we can figure out a way to do that as a nation, as well as individuals, there might be an answer.

Best, Kathleen

Present in Our Space

A Meditation on the Meaning of Slave Tags

An article in *The Seattle Times*[1] piqued my curiosity about a branch of collecting. During the time of legal slavery in the United States, slaveholders in South Carolina were allowed to rent their slaves to other individuals, or even municipalities. A slave owner would pay the city a fee to rent their slaves, much as one pays a car license fee.

In order that they might be readily identified, these people were issued metal "slave tags," a sort of badge that bore a number and the task that the wearer was designated to perform, such as "house servant" or "mechanic." Slave owners were fined if the slave failed to wear the tag. It enabled him or her to walk alone through the city, or be put to work outside of the context of a plantation. This method of identification was in use for only a short time, so not too many tags were issued.

Now, they are sought as collector's items, bringing as much as $26,000 at auction.

"People like the rarity," says Harlan Greene, coauthor of a forthcoming book on the slave badges. "But I also think it is the drama, the Gothic horror in that it was worn by a slave."[2]

My first question upon reading this article was, Who would collect these? I went on eBay (for the first time!) and sure enough, there were three lots that included these tags for sale, all by the same seller. I was also reminded that people collect African Americana — Aunt Jemima syrup containers, and Little Golden Books about Little Black Sambo. I recalled reading an article about this, a younger generation of African Americans intrigued by the objectification of their coloring and culture. *The Art and History of Black Memorabilia*[3] covers this field of collecting, and there is even a *Black Ethnic Collectibles*[4] magazine.

But slave tags? I imagined trying to ask my parents, Mexican immigrants, about something like this, knowing they would recoil at the thought. They would see no irony in it. How do you even write about the trappings of slavery without being pulled under by the horror of it? I felt that sense of dread return that I felt while trying to write about the murder trial of Andrea Yates. I put off writing this piece.

But during a recent class I taught at Richard Hugo House, Walter Benjamin told me something vitally important, something I have struggled with for ten years of my own writing.

On page 206 of *The Arcades Project*[5] he writes, "The true method of making things present is to represent them in our space (not to represent ourselves in their space). . . . We don't displace our being into theirs; they step into our life."

In order to talk about slave tags, I must detach them from the context of the antebellum South, bring them forward (a little dirt still clinging to them, as in the catalogue descriptions), and objectify them. I must view them with the cool eye of the flaneur—the unencumbered, unrushed stroller of Benjamin's Paris—and describe them as I would a Hummel doll or a shell.

Is that right? Benjamin, a secularized Jew who perished while trying to escape Nazi-occupied France, offers another clue that I puzzled over late one night, looking up the term in both the English and French dictionaries. The term was *quodlibet*. The *American Heritage Dictionary* defines it as "1. a. A theological or philosophical issue presented for formal argument or disputation. b. The disputation itself."[6] *LaRousse's* French/English Dictionary, spelling it *quolibet*, defines it as "quibble, jibe."[7]

The next morning, I realized the practical definition. It was the sort of philosophical discussion that engaged medieval scholars in weeks, even months, of heated discussions, such as, "How many angels can dance on the head of a pin?" It must be the source of the term *quibble*, which we think of as arguing over an insubstantial detail.

In trying to understand slave tags, I had stumbled onto a quodlibet, a set of concrete objects that could only spark endless rounds of political, social, cultural, and moral discussion. There was no one answer to the question "Why would someone collect slave tags?" anymore than there is a simple answer to the question "How could anyone keep slaves?"

I doubt that most collectors read such import into their collections, whether they involve buttons, baseball cards, or African American memorabilia, but by taking objects out of their original context and placing them under the spotlight, so to speak, of a collector's eye, it allows us to see these objects in a new way, and perhaps bring to bear our newer sensibilities onto their original intent.

Since its inception, eBay has been forced to pull objects from auction for a variety of reasons, most often because visitors found the objects offensive, or more interestingly, found the idea of trafficking in these objects offensive. By default, eBay has become a reflection of popular taste and sensibilities. You know someone has sunk too low when their offering is pulled from eBay.

But as I thought about the long list of restrictions, activities, and identifications with which we are saddled in a post–9/11 world, the idea of slave tags came to have more relevance. If airlines can screen us by our credit card accounts before allowing us to board a plane, or libraries are forced to share our reading tastes with Homeland Security, then the modern equivalent of slave tags is not far behind.

I read recently about an elementary school on the East Coast that was using retinal scans to screen adult visitors. In the same newspaper, it was suggested that DNA testing could be used to identify some of the thousands who have perished trying to cross the Mexican-U.S. border in order to find work, their bleached bones discovered, sometimes years later, in the Chihuahuan and Sonoran deserts. DNA sampling has been used for some time to identify the "worthy" dead, such as those lost in combat, but has not yet been used to identify the anonymous poor who were not yet wearing their slave tags.

Ironically (there's that word again), the use of slave tags in South Carolina disappeared, in part, due to the objections of free-white laborers. Because the slaves were usually skilled labor, free whites felt that they were competing with slaves, who, since they received none of the income anyway, could be rented for a lower amount than one would pay a free-white laborer. That's why the slave tags are rare.

It won't be long before most of us have a little card or tag that will literally open borders or doors for us, or allow us to purchase groceries — oh right, that already happens. But the question remains, will these tags mark us as masters of our situation, or slaves to it? Regrettably, the numbers that correspond to the letters for Homeland Security don't add up to 666, but I won't let that quodlibet get in my way — the mark of the beast, now liberated from its place as a designation of a rural highway, will soon be upon us.

∴ VI ∴

The Woman Who Loved Water

Among the Living

It was the chance of a lifetime. The University of Texas–Pan American asked me to visit, and so I got out a map of the United States and Mexico in order to see where, exactly, Edinburg, Texas, might be. Sure enough, as distances go in the West, it was very close to Saltillo.

I didn't have much time. I spoke in Texas on a Thursday and Friday, then got on a bus to Saltillo around 2:30 PM. It was 10:30 before the bus rolled into the station. By then, it was full of workers from Monterrey anxious to get home for the weekend. Four single women and a middle-aged man with his mother had ridden the bus all the way from Reynosa with me, one with a small boy. That last stretch over the mountains, an older man with a large, framed picture, a rolled rug, and an extremely runny nose sat in the seat next to me. While I often speak to strangers on my travels (after all, I am the stranger!) I did not have a conversation with him.

The last passage over the mountains was dark and eerie. There had been rain in the area ever since I had arrived, and now it appeared to be snowing through my foggy window. What if it's snowing in Saltillo? I thought. I was wearing sandals.

A brightly lit complex of buildings loomed out of the darkness, a mine or a factory, I thought. Later I found out it was a power plant. More buildings appeared, until it was clear we were in the suburbs of Saltillo. Not a soul was to be seen on the streets, except for a boy of around ten painting graffiti on a wall. A huge ad for condoms, showing a satisfied, postcoital woman, greeted us. She was mostly dressed. This was, after all, Mexico.

A woman who had befriended me in Reynosa shared her cab and directed the driver to my hotel. We drove through a dizzying maze of narrow, cobblestoned streets in the pouring rain. In my fatigue, I despaired of ever finding my way around the next day, my only day in Saltillo.

But the next morning, the sun was shining. The hotel restaurant had my favorite breakfast — *frutas de estación*, yogurt, granola, and coffee. The bell boy, whom I had accidentally overtipped the night before in my efforts to get rid of him, filled my hands with brochures of things to see and do. I set out.

The third person I spoke with was a relative.

"Does a woman live here who is a Narro?" I asked in my awkward Spanish.

"Yes," said a man at a wrought-iron gate, "and I am, too. I'm her brother." He opened the gate and invited me in.

A central image in my writing, an image from my childhood, is looking into a gated courtyard with a fountain at its center. I was two when I last visited Saltillo. I was told that we could not go in, because this place no longer belonged to our family. The complications of time, religion, inheritance, and disinheritance were beyond me then, and I still struggle to understand how we choose to shape our long-term relationships with others.

So the gate opening, and my cousin Manuel Eduardo Moreira y Narro inviting me in, were very special. While we waited for his sister to comb out her hair, Manuel introduced me to their aunt, María Moreira, who is bedridden. She turns ninety-five this month, and intends to live to be one hundred.

Amalia Moreira Narro de Heede and her American husband, Fritz Heede, then invited me into the main house. Ownership of the house is complicated, but for now, they live there part-time, helping to care for the aunt.

The three of them told me many stories. They did not mind that I took notes. I tried not to be overwhelmed with names and dates, with the fact that the stories my branch of the family craved were the fabric of their everyday lives. Besides the privately published book of the family's history, there was a reunion a few years ago at El Morillo, a nearby *rancho* that now serves as a resort, still owned by some of the family. We did not know about it, and I think how my cousin Miguel, my grandfather's namesake, would have loved to have been there. He had died a year before my visit.

There is no fountain in this courtyard — was it the same one I visited as a child? — but Manuel showed me that, if you stand at a certain distance, an image of the Virgin Mary can be seen in the hollow of a tree. Near it are deep-pink roses with a swoony perfume. He clearly delights in the garden.

And now I have more stories to tell. This time, with the help of the many Narros who never severed the ties that were loosened so long ago, when my eighteen-year-old grandfather spent the night in the train station, alone and rejected, asking God to guide his life.

The Woman Who Loved Water

Once, there was a woman who loved water. On dry land, she could merely walk. But in the water, she could fly. She spent as much time as possible in the water, and that is where her husband first saw her — floating on her back in a swimming pool, completely at ease. He vowed to meet her, and eventually, they were married.

The two of them were very happy, and they wanted to have many children. The woman continued to swim until her first child was born. For a time after that, the water seemed to whisper unfamiliar things to her, strange things, but she did not listen. After their second child was born, the water began to whisper again, more strongly this time, but the woman stopped her ears and said "No, no, no!" until the whispers receded. The woman loved her children very much.

Her husband proposed that they free themselves of earthly possessions, that they live simply and concentrate on their family. They sold their home and most of their possessions and moved to a small trailer. But they were near the water, and so the woman was happy.

After the birth of their third child, the waters in her head came back more strongly. She had to concentrate to block out what the voices were saying. It was exhausting, scary. She confessed to her husband that it was hard to be with three children in such a small space, to care for them by herself while he was gone all day, to teach them and cook for them and clean.

And so, the family moved closer to his parents. They bought a house. The waters in her mind receded, and the woman was happy again. A fourth child was born. The waters surged forward, as though waiting, waiting for her. In order to hold back the whispers, to keep their meaning from becoming obvious, the woman had to concentrate all her energy on the breaking waves in her head. She could no longer eat. She could no longer sleep. She could no longer care for her children. The man took her to a doctor, who gave her medicine. The doctor told the husband that the woman would be all right, that the water in her head was only temporary, but that it was strongest when she had just had a child. The doctor suggested that they have no more children.

But they did. And with the fifth child, the dam that the woman had so carefully constructed between her mind and the black, surging waters finally broke. She could no longer hold them back, nor could she ignore what the whispers had been trying to tell her all along. She finally listened to the voices, and did as they told her. The woman filled the bathtub and drowned her five children.

"   ⋅:⋅ ⋅:⋅ ⋅:⋅ ⋅:⋅ ⋅:⋅

This is a terrible story, based on an account of Andrea Yates's murder of her children in *Time* magazine. "She was a person who was more graceful in the water than out of it," said her husband, Russell (Rusty) Yates.[1] I read about the case and heard about it and flinched with each additional detail. I scrutinized her photograph in the paper to see what I could discern about her state of mind from her appearance. The whole thing seemed unbelievable.

But there was something disturbingly familiar about this tale, as well.

One day, I realized why. I have been hearing this story, in one form or another, all my life.

One version goes like this: Once there was a woman who fell in love with a man. He was very handsome, and all the women desired him. Eventually, she attracted his notice and they were married. They were very happy, or so she thought, and had many children. One day, the woman went to the river to get water and saw her husband with another woman. In a fit of rage and jealousy, she drowned all of her children. She was put to death for her crime, but continues to haunt the river, looking for her lost children. She can be heard late at night, weeping.

This is, of course, the most famous of Mexican folktales, the story of La Llorona, the weeping woman. There have been songs written about her, and there are many versions of the stories and the songs, with echoes of her undying love for both the children and the absent father.

"How does a person survive who cannot speak up to explain what she wants," asks Rosemarie Coste in "La Llorona y El Grito/ The Ghost and The Scream: Noisy Women in Borderlands and Beyond," her exploration of the Llorona myths and their interpretation, "who cannot argue when she is pushed in a direction she does not want to go, who cannot insist that she be consulted when decisions are made about her future?"[2]

This seems to describe Andrea Yates, a woman wracked by mental illness, in a marriage based on the fundamentalist teachings of Michael Woroniecki, a preacher unaffiliated with any established religious group who traveled around the country in a camper with his wife, Rachel, and six children, often speaking at college campuses, and homeschooling his children.

Russell Yates admired this lifestyle. "Man is the breadwinner and woman is the homemaker," he told prosecutor Joe Owmby under cross-examination at Andrea Yates's trial. "It's the way it's been for years." Social worker Earline Wilcott, who counseled Andrea Yates for years, testified that she met Russell Yates once and learned that his beliefs included that a wife should submit to her husband.[3] This belief is based on Ephesians 5:22–24: "Wives, be subject to your own husbands, as to the Lord. For the husband is the head of the wife, as Christ also is the head of the church. . . . But as the church is subject to Christ, so also the wives ought to be to their husbands in everything."[4] These few verses have been the subject of much discussion over the years, as women have struggled to reach religious parity with men. Both sides usually ignore the instructions to men that follow.

A more sinister view of women, however, shows up in Woroniecki's teachings: "Woroniecki preached a stern and patriarchal doctrine. In letters and taped messages to the [Yates] family, he claimed 'all women are descendants of Eve and Eve was a witch. The women, particularly women who worked outside the home, are wicked.'"[5] The Yateses purchased Woroniecki's old motor home, with 350 square feet of living space in which to live, in 1998. Only after Andrea attempted suicide twice, and at her parents' insistence, did they move back into a house in Houston.[6]

Andrea Yates had worked as a post-op nurse at M. D. Anderson Cancer Center before she met Russell and until the birth of her first child, and continued to act as a caregiver for her father, who had Alzheimer's and had never fully recovered from a heart attack. Her father, Andrew Kennedy, died a few months after the birth of Andrea's last child, Mary, and shortly before her last breakdown.[7]

La Llorona weeps wordlessly, "unspeakably," Coste continues, "expressing her longing for the precious things she has lost and cannot find: her home, her family, her body, her life. The many versions of her story differ as to what her losses were and how they occurred, but they unite in judging her to be certainly miserable and probably dangerous, jealous of those who still have the treasures she long ago lost."[8]

When Yates was hospitalized with postpartum depression, her friend Debbie Holmes testified, Russell could not understand why his wife couldn't keep up with taking care of the children and home-schooling them. He admired another woman in the neighborhood: "She's got nine kids, teaches her kids tee ball, and she does just fine. I don't know why Andrea's having so much trouble," said Russell Yates, according to Holmes.[9]

"A woman who will not suffer silently, who makes her displeasure heard and expects it to be dealt with, is an exceptional and amazing creature in a culture like the one that created La llorona's legend, a culture that values patient endurance above many other virtues."[10]

In *Borderlands/La Frontera*, Gloria Anzaldúa writes extensively about attempts to silence the Chicana, the mixed-blood Latinas of the border between Mexico and the United States.

> *En boca cerrada no entran moscas.* "Flies don't enter a closed mouth" is a saying I kept hearing when I was a child. *Ser habladora* was to be a gossip and a liar, to talk too much. *Muchachitas bien criadas*, well-bred girls don't answer back. *Es una falta de respeto* to talk back to one's mother or father . . . *hablar pa' trás, repelar, hocicona, repelona, chismosa*, having a big mouth, questioning, carrying tales are all signs of being *mal criada*. In my culture they are all words that are derogatory if applied to women — I've never heard them applied to men.[11]

Anzaldúa is one of the few people who has attempted to rewrite the Llorona myth, in her children's book *Prietita and the Ghost*

Woman/Prietita y la llorona,[12] which features a benevolent Llorona guiding a lost girl, first to a medicinal herb for her mother, then to rescue. Interestingly, this ghost woman is completely silent.

While there are many differences between Andrea Yates's situation and those of Latina women, the fundamental Christian belief system to which she adheres values the wife who submits to her husband, and there is some indication that this was true of the Yates family.

Frank Ochberg, MD, a psychiatrist and the author of *Post-Traumatic Therapy and Victims of Violence*,[13] said in a talk in Seattle that the first sign of trauma is speechlessness. Most violence is in the home, he says, and so is especially difficult to treat. "If the language of the victim or advocate is too strong," he says, "ears close. If it is too soft, it is not heard."[14]

Sandra Cisneros also retells the Llorona myth in her story "Woman Hollering Creek." In it, Cleofílas finds the voice to tell a health worker of her abusive situation, and is rescued by a woman who, "when they drove across the *arroyo* . . . opened her mouth and let out a yell as loud as any mariachi.

"'I like the name of that *arroyo*,' she tells her startled passenger. 'Makes you want to holler like Tarzan, right?'"[15] In this case, Cisneros shows that the silence of abuse can be escaped, and the legend reimagined to show a woman who stands up for herself.

There is no indication that Andrea Yates ever complained about her situation, or even saw herself in that light. The worst that was put in writing was that "the patient's husband might be a little bit controlling."[16] Rather, according to Sergeant Eric Mehl, the officer who responded to her 911 call and took her confession, "She would sit in 15 seconds of stone-cold silence if he asked too much. She could give only short answers to simple questions in their 17-minute conversation as she twice recounted the order in which her children were born and died."[17]

⁂ ⁂ ⁂ ⁂ ⁂

Another version of La Llorona goes like this: a man and a woman fell in love and married. They were very happy, but very poor. They did not have enough food or money to feed their children, and so the man left their village to look for work. The woman was left alone with the children, and, after the man had been gone a long time, they began to starve to death. Finally, the woman drowned her children in the river rather than watch them starve. To this day, she grieves, and can be heard calling for them along the riverbank, looking for her lost children. You can hear her there, calling late at night, and if she mistakes you for one of her children, she might take you, too. I was told this version in the 1970s by a college classmate, the daughter of farmworkers, who went on to become a lawyer for the Mexican American Legal Defense Fund.

On June 20, 2001, Andrea Yates, 37, told Officer Eric Mehl that she drowned her five children — Noah, 7, John, 5, Paul, 3, Luke, 2, and 6-month-old Mary.

Three weeks later, she told psychiatrist Phillip Resnick that she was failing as a mother and believed she had to kill the children to keep them from going to hell. "These were their innocent years," she told him. "God would take them up."[18]

Yates drowned her children to save them from eternal damnation. Because she had been a bad mother, she reasoned, her children were also turning out to be bad. Only by drowning them while they were still young and innocent, by sacrificing herself to the laws of secular man, could she assure their eternal salvation. She, in turn, would be executed by the state and Satan would be eliminated from the world.

"I realized it was time to be punished," Yates told Sgt. Eric Mehl.

"And what do you need to be punished for?"

"For not being a good mother."[19]

After her imprisonment, Yates told doctors that the death of her children was *her* punishment, not theirs. It was, she explained, a mother's final act of mercy. According to the Bible, it was better to be flung into the sea with a stone tied to one's neck than cause little ones to stumble.[20] And she had failed them.

This is an important point in Yates's system of belief. It had been her job to instruct her children, both in secular studies and in religious studies, since the Yateses did not attend church. Rather, they held Bible studies three evenings a week. Yates had "earmarked pages in her Bible about a mother's obligation to raise her children or face the consequences. . . . She came to believe that she had failed so badly to measure up to her own extreme ideals of motherhood (she thought the kids should say their ABCs by age 2) that, as she told the psychiatrist, the kids were destined to perish in the fires of hell."[21]

Hamida Bosmajian, a professor of English at Seattle University, has made a study of the use of language in the indoctrination of children by the Nazi regime. During the Third Reich, power was achieved primarily by the use of language. First, it was used to divide people from each other, then to unite those who were left. "Children in particular were reshaped as warriors," said Bosmajian. They were told that individual identity counted for nothing. Finally, the general population was encouraged to "become like children" and let the people in power maintain the material conditions of life.[22]

Only by making sure that her young children were well-versed in the beliefs of their elders could they become warriors for Christ. If they could not read the Bible, this would not be possible. "They did a lot of silly stuff and didn't obey," Yates said. "They did things God didn't like."[23]

Because Andrea Yates was unable to do all that was expected of her, she was a bad mother. Because she was a bad mother, her children were bad. Only her execution would rescue them from the evil inside her — a state-sanctioned exorcism in which George W. Bush, the former governor and now president, would come to save her from the clutches of Satan.[24]

In the last days before the drownings, Yates had also wanted to have her head shaved so that she could see the mark of the beast as described in the Book of Revelation,[25] the number 666, that she was sure was emblazoned on her scalp.

After Yates's arrest, Michael Woroniecki tried to downplay the influence he had on the family through personal correspondence and through his publication, *The Perilous Times*, a copy of which was put into evidence by Yates's attorney.[26] In it, a poem laments the disobedient children of the "Modern Mother Worldly," ending with the question, "What becomes of the children of such a Jezebel?" Woroniecki wrote a letter to *Newsweek* magazine denying responsibility for Yates's actions. But his views of women were shared by Russell Yates, who saw his wife's mental illness as an indication that her resistance to evil had been lowered.

At one point when court-appointed psychiatrist Phillip Resnick was interviewing Yates, he asked her how she felt about her children.

"I didn't hate my children," she responded.

"Did you love your children?" Resnick asked.

"Yeah," she responded after a long pause. "Some. Not in the right way, though."[27]

According to Coste, folklorists claim to see, in the hundreds of variants of the La Llorona tale, "Mexican-American cultural attitudes toward mothering activities and . . . the conflicts and stresses that Mexican-American women experience in relation to the mother role," as well as "insight into the interpretation of the infanticide motif as a psychological device related to the frustrations of child care," showing that "contemplation of infanticide provides a momentary 'escape' from the problems of child rearing."[28]

Like all living mythology, there are newer versions of La Llorona. Coste has found "the first signs of a merging of the traditional La Llorona legend and the contemporary stories of babies found abandoned in trash dumpsters, a more modern method for disposing of children than drowning."[29]

Coste also found research showing that La Llorona is known to the female inmates of juvenile hall, even by those who do not know her by name. Of thirty-one ghost stories collected by researcher Bess Lomax Hawes, twenty-eight were about adult women, most of whom were threats to the living. This is in contrast to ghost lore in general, in which most ghosts are males who are indifferent to the living. The girls' stories varied in many details, but all featured ghosts that were female, vicious, and very much inclined to attack. The most frequent themes were infanticide and other aggressive crimes committed by women, punishment or aggressive crimes against women, inconsolable grief or loss, and mutilation, another kind of loss.[30]

Of the two versions of La Llorona I have recounted here, I suspect that men are more likely to tell the first version — of the woman who drowns her children for spite — and women the second — the woman who drowns her children to spare them suffering. One is a story of jealousy, and the second, a story of desperation. One could argue that, if La Llorona killed her children out of spite and jealousy, she did it for the wrong reasons. If she killed her children out of pity and mercy, then she did it for the right reasons — still wrong, but motivated by compassion.

"Even though she knew it was against the law," said psychiatrist

Phillip Resnick, "she did what she thought was right in the world she perceived through her psychotic eyes at the time."[31]

Which version is closer to the truth? And which model did the jury have in mind when they convicted Andrea Yates of murder on March 12, 2002? Under Texas law Yates "could have been found not guilty only if jurors believed she suffered from a mental defect that prevented her from distinguishing right from wrong."[32] The jury took less than four hours to reach a verdict. During the deliberations, the jury requested an audiotape player and may have listened again to the 911 recording of Andrea Yates's call to the police and her taped confession. This suggests that they concentrated on her actions the morning of the killings, rather than the extensive testimony describing her history of mental illness.

"The way she did it and the way she acted afterwards was inconsistent with somebody who didn't know what she was doing," said Rusty Hardin, a former local prosecutor who watched closing arguments.[33]

In the Llorona tales, the townspeople feel the same way. In some versions, she is stoned or hung by the other villagers when it is discovered what she has done. In others, she stays by the river and wastes away on her own, until only the wail is left.

"The loving act of a mother was to leave [Noah's] body floating in the bathtub," said prosecuting attorney Raylynn Williford, sarcastically, in closing arguments. "She made the choice to fill the tub. She made the choice to kill these children. She knew it was wrong. . . .

"At one point during Ms. Williford's arguments, Mrs. Yates cried silently at the defense table."[34]

Sadly, Noah was named after the biblical patriarch to whom God made the promise that the world would never again be destroyed by water.[35]

What is La Llorona trying to tell us? And why is the Andrea Yates case so eerily similar?

Tales of the supernatural persist because they portray a situation that we continue to understand over the passage of time and place. They carry some universal meaning that allows them to be adapted to current circumstances, always timely, always applicable. The specific characters may change, but as editor Rob Johnson says in the introduction to *Fantasmas: Supernatural Stories by Mexican American Writers*, these stories "never forget there is a spiritual side of life, but even more importantly, don't ignore social reality."[36]

La Llorona is, in part, a story about power — power over our own circumstances. What control do we have over what happens to us, over what happens to the closest thing that we have to an extension of ourselves, our children? The song versions of La Llorona, in particular, tell us that she was dark: "*Todos me dicen el negro, llorona/Negro pero cariñoso.*"

And so most likely, lower class and powerless. Some versions of the Llorona story, those that fall into the jealous-woman category, also say that she is lower class, and her husband/lover is of the upper class. But she is also reminiscent of the beautiful lover in the Song of Songs:

I am dark, but comely . . .
Don't stare at me because I am swarthy,
Because the sun has gazed upon me.[37]

What does a middle-class Anglo woman, supposedly living in comfortable circumstances, have in common with a poor, dark woman from Mexico? These questions continued to haunt me as I traveled to Texas and Mexico in April 2002, closer to the origin of the Llorona stories.

❖ ❖ ❖ ❖ ❖

In Saltillo, Mexico, I took the opportunity to ask a couple of people their version of La Llorona. It turned out to be quite different from that recounted in the United States.

My cousin, Amalia Moreira Narro de Heede, who is in her seventies, told me a version she had heard from her great-grandmother on her mother's side. This is a pre-Hispanic version, she said. In it, a woman had a premonition that the Spaniards were coming to Mexico and would slaughter her children. She began to cry, "*¡Ay, mis hijos! Ay, mis hijos!*" She appeared in a long white dress, with long hair to the ground.

On the plane to Houston, I asked a man, who appeared to be in his late thirties, if he had heard the Llorona story. He was reading an

American murder mystery in Spanish. He said that he was originally from Reynosa, Mexico, but worked in McAllen. The man put down his book and thought a minute. He said that his grandmother used to read a lot, and liked to tell them stories. Yes, he said, he had heard about a woman in a white dress calling "*Ay, mis hijos, ay, mis hijos,*" because her children had died. He could not remember why they had died, or how.

As I thought about it, the long white dress gave me a clue: the priests and holy people in the court of Moctezuma wore long white gowns, and were not allowed to cut their hair. It was caked from dried blood due to their almost daily ritual of bloodletting. The image of the woman was a warning to others, like the warnings of the dreamers disregarded by Moctezuma until it was too late. This Llorona starts to sound a lot like the dreamers in Ana Castillo's *Massacre of the Dreamers: Essays on Xicanisma:*

> Moteuczoma [*sic*] called upon the thousands of dreamers who were sharing the same premonition: the prophesied arrival of Cortés and the subsequent annihilation of the Empire. Moteuc-zoma's order to have the dreamers murdered en masse did not stop the landing of those alien ships that were already on their way. . . .
>
> Moteuczoma, who relied heavily on mysticism and having re-ceived various ominous omens about the fall of his empire, also consulted with his greatest wizards and magicians. These, unable to advise Moteuczoma as to how to prevent what had already been divinely decreed were imprisoned. But being magicians they mysteriously escaped. Moteuczoma avenged them by having their wives and children hung and their houses destroyed.[38]

Nearly the entire time that I was in Texas and Mexico, it rained. They told me it had not rained for months, and my relatives began to call me Tlaloc, the rain god, because I had brought rain from the Northwest. Like columnist Patricia Gonzales, in her essay of March 8, 2002, "I carry a pot of tears on my head. . . . La Llorona tells us there is something wrong with society, that there are many forms of madness."[39] It occurred to me, as I jumped across puddles in my sandals, that the drownings of these children, in Andrea Yates's universe, might have been a sort of baptism. Romans 6:4 encourages us to be "buried with Him through baptism into death, in order that as Christ was raised from the dead through the glory of the Father, so we too might walk in newness of life."[40] In her attempt to save her children from her own madness and powerlessness, Yates may have taken the only tangible step that promised salvation at the time.

After a spectacular lightning storm the night before, my last morning in Saltillo dawned calm and sunny. I turned on the shower to warm up the water before getting in. When it still seemed cool, I gave it a few more seconds. That's when I heard a noise near the ceiling and instinctively ducked away from the open shower door. An enormous crash followed. When I looked around, the shower was filled with the wet, sparkling shards of a huge light fixture that had detached from the ceiling and broken to bits on the concrete shower floor.

"We have, at this point, some hope and expectation that Ms. Yates will receive the same or better care than she received before she was arrested," said Joe Lovelace, a public policy consultant for the National Alliance for the Mentally Ill of Texas. "That's not saying a lot."[41]

I may never fully comprehend why a woman who loved water drowned her own children, but I will take it as a warning that "it is not [La Llorona] who will 'get' us if we are not careful, but our own ordinary and dangerous lives."[42] I suspect that Andrea Yates's story will be added to the La Llorona lore of Texas. The old stories persist because the old ills persist. And the old ills persist because, in the end, human nature does not change.

(A Texas appeals court in early 2005 reversed the capital murder convictions of Andrea Yates. She now resides in a state-run, maximum-security mental hospital.)

The Girl in the Tree

On Rereading *Green Mansions*

When I was a little girl, I lived, for a year, in a tree. It was a very fine tree, a crape myrtle, and just the right height for spying on our neighborhood in San Bernardino without alarming people. My piercing, two-noted whistle could be heard up and down the street as I summoned Bobby or Anita Lotz to play.

This was a time of transition in our family. My father had been superintendent of the Optimist Boys' Ranch in Devore Heights for the previous five years. Following an incident in which the board of directors had held a dinner on the grounds of the ranch and had gotten drunk in front of the boys, and my father had objected, he lost his job. The Ranch was closed within a year, since it was also perceived to be bleeding off money from a similar facility that was closer to Los Angeles.

As a result, my family sold our house in rural Devore, and moved into the closest city, San Bernardino, so that my father could begin substitute teaching in the public schools. By then, my older sisters were attending schools in town, so it was probably seen as a convenience for all.

I was about six when we moved to that rented house at 447 West 21st Street. It was a beautiful house, full of built-in cupboards and light. There was a huge black walnut tree in the back, a jungle of bamboo, and a fruit cellar that, my father pointed out, could be used as a bomb shelter. It was also in a friendly neighborhood, where people held potlucks and we lived next door to a judge. Now it would be called a neighborhood in transition, but then it was just a mix of old residents and new, big houses and little, whites, a Chinese family, a Lebanese woman, and us.

Those were hard times for my parents, since money was scarce, and there were often arguments about it. I remember trying to listen to a conversation in the kitchen behind a closed door, which earned me a black eye when my father suddenly opened it and inadvertently hit me with the doorknob. A lady appeared on television with a rare folk instrument called a *ukelin*, lamenting the fact that the strings were irreplaceable. We had a ukelin, so my mother wrote and offered to sell her the strings from ours. She didn't answer.

So I loved my tree. Although on the street for all to see, it was the closest thing to my own room. I read in it. I napped in it. And although I did not spend the night in it, I probably would have if allowed to.

∴ ∴ ∴ ∴ ∴

It was some years later that I read *Green Mansions*,[1] by W. H. Hudson. It seems to me that there was some link between my reading it and my life in a tree. Perhaps someone, knowing this about me, had recommended the book. If so, this was probably in college, where people recommended books to each other. I don't remember much of that before then. However, I know I was young enough that *Green Mansions* made a deep and terrible impression on me, so searing that only now, in my middle years, have I gone back to see why this book would have affected me so profoundly.

William Henry Hudson was born August 4, 1841, in Argentina to American parents. They had moved there from Massachusetts because it provided a favorable climate for his father's tuberculosis. William himself grew up mostly self-educated, and expected to lead the life of a naturalist and adventurer, until rheumatic fever in his teens made it clear he would never lead an active life. At the age of thirty-three, according to Amy D. Ronner in *W. H. Hudson: The Man, the Novelist, the Naturalist*,[2] he moved to England, married, and wrote over twenty books of natural history, memoir, and adventure. But his most famous, still available in numerous editions, remains *Green Mansions*.

First published in 1904, *Green Mansions* is the adventure story of a young man named Abel from Venezuela who, fearing for his life following a botched political coup, leaves all behind to explore the territories of the Guyanas, south of Venezuela proper. He follows the Amazon and its tributaries upstream, living with various indigenous groups, until he meets a "savage" (Hudson employs this term a lot) wearing a necklace made of pounded disks of gold. The savage tells him (our adventurer is very good at languages) of a place where all the inhabitants wear such necklaces, and he is off on the quest that will change his life forever.

Upon reaching the Parahuaris, Abel finds neither gold nor mountains, just some low hills and some lower savages who nevertheless allow him to stick around and build them a guitar. He becomes both friend and rival to one member of the tribe, Kua-kó, and is mothered by an old woman. This, along with his nifty blue cloak, his knife, and his pistol, give him the confidence to venture into an adjacent forest that is avoided by his band of savage friends. They tell him that "the daughter of the Didi" lives there, and allows no hunting. If a spear were to be thrown or a dart shot, she would catch it and send it back against the hunter.

All of this was well and good, so far. It did bother my younger self that Abel seemed to have so little regard for the people who helped him along the way. Then he finds Rima, and falls in love with her. Better than the daughter of the Didi, Rima turns out to be a real live girl who lives in the forest, protects the animals within it, and saves him from snakebite. She is extraordinarily beautiful, and bears no resemblance to any indigenous forest dweller ever before seen in the Amazon. She is singular, a sort of "Ishi, the Last of His Tribe" before Ishi's story had been told.

The problem, of course, was that I fell head over heels in love with the idea of Rima. Here was someone much like me, of dubious ancestry and unclassifiable appearance, down to her fuzzy halo of hair that appeared to be a different color depending on the light. She spoke a wonderful, birdlike language that Abel was unable to understand, and could travel through the treetops like a monkey. Rima lived the life I wanted to live, far from the commonplaces of California, far from the confining behavior that had been imposed on me in ever-larger doses as I grew and matured away from the girl in the tree.

Had I known anything about literature, I would have understood that calling the indigenous people "savages" was a foreshadowing of the end: The people who shelter Abel during his sojourn eventually kill Rima in order to gain access to her forest.

When I got to this part of the story I was so upset that I barely made it through the rest of the book to the end. In fact, I may not have made it to the end. I probably read just as far as Abel gathering her bones so that, in death, they might mingle with his. Once her death was incontrovertibly confirmed in the book, I think I abandoned it. Only now have I gone back to try to understand why Rima had to die.

Hudson, by portraying Rima as the last of her mysterious people, makes it clear that there is not room in a modern world for such gentle souls. Her own mother is found injured by Rima's guardian, Nuflo, an old man who until that point has lived the life of an outlaw, and who rescues her from his more bloodthirsty cohorts. He realizes that she is expecting a child, and convinces her to travel with him to a village where women can help her with her delivery. Lame from her injury, Rima's mother alternately pines for her lost people and teaches Rima their unique language. She wastes away, apparently from the unhealthy climate, and before dying, convinces Nuflo to take Rima to a higher altitude, where she has a chance of surviving. Thus they come to live in the isolated forest where Abel finds them.

I reread this book at the age of 48, lying on the shore of glacier-fed Wallowa Lake in eastern Oregon. In a box canyon isolated enough to generate its own mythology, Wallowa feels as innocent as Rima's paradise, where protected deer move among the tourists like life-size audio-animatronics from Disneyland, and the water is the purest I have ever tasted. One could easily imagine the bird girl flitting near the mountain trails, moving from tree to tree as effortlessly as the butterflies.

Yet here, too, has been ugliness. The white settlers evicted the Nez Percé from Chief Joseph's resting place and told them never to return. Horace Axtell's grandmother grew up here, and he remembers watching her weep, too respectful to ask why. Horace and his wife, Andrea, are now allowed to visit as guests of Fishtrap, a writers' conference, where Horace teaches the Nez Percé language to eager white students. He seems to bear no grudges, but is thankful for each moment he spends in this place of magic.

∴ ∴ ∴ ∴ ∴

In *Green Mansions*, Hudson describes an indifferent God, a God who does not reward good nor punish evil, but looks upon both with an equally jaundiced eye. He describes Nuflo's hopes for divine intervention by Rima's deceased mother, and Rima's prayers to that same mother, in the same childish terms as he describes the superstitions that the Indians have about Rima and her enchanted forest.

By taking her to the land of her birth and source of her name, Riolama, Abel carefully kills Rima's spiritual ties to her past, the expectation that there might be others like her with whom she can converse in her "true" language. This yearning for the missing others reminded me of Zena Henderson's novels about the descendants of a group of space travelers who crash-land on earth.[3] They intermarry with the locals, so that their children inherit supernatural traits here and there. But the books are suffused with an intense longing for the unknown community, the wholeness of a culture that has been handed down in bits and pieces. Only when disabused of her unrealistic notions does Rima awaken to Abel's carnal passions. There is a section in the book during which she slowly returns from the brink of death. As Abel holds her in his arms, the color gradually returns to her lips until Abel cannot refrain from kissing them, and she does not resist. It is, metaphorically, a description of her first orgasm. Only then does she call him by his name.

Like Mary Shelley before him in *Frankenstein*,[4] first published in 1818, Hudson has breathed life into a monster. An ethnically ambiguous woman in complete harmony with nature, unfettered by church or civilization in her newly awakened sexuality, cannot be allowed to live in such a book. W. H. Hudson's readers could not have accepted this violation of the natural order of things, anymore than could Hudson himself. As a respected naturalist specializing in the birds of England and South America, Hudson described the social and ethnic differences among his fictional human characters with the same particularity as he did the flora and fauna in his nonfiction.

Rima's abandonment of her hopes leads her to trust Abel and return to her forest to wait for him. It is there that she is struck down "like a great white bird killed with an arrow and falling to the earth, and it fell into the flames beneath," perishing in the huge conflagration built around her tree by the Indians.[5] The balance of faiths is destroyed by the nonbeliever Abel's involvement, yet he survives all. The series of events is described as the inexorable march of progress — regrettable, but nevertheless, unavoidable.

This theme is echoed in Hudson's other adventure books, such as *The Purple Land*[6] and *The Crystal Age*,[7] in which he describes the potential pairings of ideal women and mere mortals, each of which is cut short before consummation. At least in *The Crystal Age*, it is the man who dies.

∴ ∴ ∴ ∴ ∴

When I first read *Green Mansions*, I did not know anything about archetypes or stereotypes. I had begun reading science fiction at an early age because I found *Have Spacesuit, Will Travel*,[8] by Robert A. Heinlein, in a school library, and it had a female protagonist, albeit one who behaved oddly. By the time I was twelve, *Star Trek*,[9] bless their pointed ears, had Lieutenant Uhuru on board, female *and* black, even if the planets they visited were all populated by blonde women in tinfoil bikinis. I had tried and failed to make sense of classics like *Pride and Prejudice*[10] — who cared what kind of gloves she was wearing? The symbols of civilization in British drawing-room dramas were more alien to me than the attributes of a good horse or a good car.

Don Quixote de la Mancha[11] I understood. Most idealists are seen as fools. But it wasn't until the essays of Joan Didion[12] that I would recognize a familiar landscape, familiar details of people whose lives ran out of gas in the anonymous cities of Southern California. The urban jungles of the New World were my home territory, and perhaps I had been waiting for literature that addressed this terrain. The works of García Márquez had not yet been translated into English — to be followed by a subsequent flood of Latin American authors in translation — and my contemporaries had not yet grown up and written our version of the world.

And yes, now I remembered. I had stopped reading *Green Man-*

sions after the Indians describe Rima's death to Abel. I hoped it was a lie, and perhaps I was afraid to find out. My freshman-year room-mate—for I read the book during my first year of college—had regarded me with the same fear and suspicion with which any respectable townswoman would have regarded Rima. Either discovering that I had not finished the book, or sensing my discomfort with it, she had insisted on reading the passages of Rima's death and the discovery of her bones out loud to me.

Why this was so important to her, I do not know, but it was certainly symptomatic of our relationship—she, the political science professor's daughter, defender of rationality and civilization; I, the half-formed creature of shadows and an alien culture, crouched at the outer edge of the collegiate campfire. (And this in spite of the fact that I had hidden her in the closet from her Mormon cousins when they came to invite her to youth activities.)

The part after Rima's death is even darker. Abel, crazed with grief, spends two months inciting a neighboring group to attack and destroy every member of the small tribe that had killed Rima. He takes part in the nighttime raid, and is only brought to his senses by the sight of the old woman who had once befriended him. He then slinks off into Rima's forest and lives hand to mouth, deep in depression and hallucinations, until he is able to kill a sloth and provision himself for a journey. Bearing Rima's bones, he makes his way back to civilization, where a convenient inheritance allows him to resume the life of a gentleman and tell this story.

While recalling the scene of Rima's death, I was reminded of a series of murals I once saw in Chihuahua. It was in an art nouveau mansion that is now a regional museum. The little girl's room was decorated with illustrations from *Little Red Riding Hood*. The story culminated with the girl and the wolf, say my notes, as "good buddies." The illustrator understood the meaning of the fairy tale very well, and it made me wonder how well acquainted he had been with the little girl. Yet the image I recall is that of a fox hiding in a great tree, only the red brush of his tail showing. The image seems to be purely a work of my own imagination, based on those murals. It is a rebus or transliteration of the phrase "burning bush."

In this image lie the three meanings I must take away from *Green Mansions*: That Rima's tree is a burning bush, her death caused by people who feared her. Like the wolf in *Little Red Riding Hood*, it is also the onset of sexuality. Finally, the burning bush was God's way of getting Moses' attention, a terrible and inescapable miracle, speaking to the inarticulate young man and telling him to demand that Pharaoh let his people go. What does Hudson's burning bush have to say to Abel, slain by his brother Cain so long ago, or to us?

There is a clue to Hudson's private iconography in *The Crystal Age*, when Smith, a traveler from Hudson's England, awakens from a fall to find himself in a utopian future society: "I regretted too late that I had not exercised more restraint; but the hungry man does not and cannot consider consequences, else a certain hairy gentleman who figures in ancient history had never lent himself to that nefarious compact, which gave so great an advantage to a younger but sleek and well-nourished brother."[13]

In that case, Hudson has split man's nature into that of the hungry, hairy individual ruled by his baser instincts, Esau, and Joseph, the more cerebral of the two brothers, who uses his wit to gain his brother's birthright. In *Green Mansions*, Abel, the product of a "civilized" society, is balanced by his adopted brother in the tribe, Kua-kó, who must play Cain. He resents Abel's easy acceptance into tribal society, and covets his gun. Eventually, he leads the assault on Rima's forest, and Abel returns to kill Kua-kó, along with the rest of the group. Abel is rewarded with material wealth, and left without the ability to form close human relationships. The preface of the story is a frame in which his friend insists on hearing Abel's story, which he has kept a secret for years. Only when pressed does he tell his tale.

Throughout his career, Hudson's ideas veered between the widespread influence of Charles Darwin's *Origin of Species*,[14] published in 1859, and utopianism. He thought the ideal was man living in complete physical and spiritual harmony with nature, yet felt that the human race was incapable of doing so until it evolved past its baser instincts — greed, war, and yes, even sexuality. In *The Crystal*

Age, Smith gives up hope of marrying his Rima-like Yoletta when he thinks that she can never share his physical passion. In *Green Mansions*, Rima becomes tainted by Abel's lust, and so loses the other-worldly advantage that had kept her safe from her neighbors.

A great deal is made in the book of Abel's pistol, which is stolen from him by Kua-kó. We are led to assume that the pistol will be turned against either Abel or Rima, but in the end, the Indians use fire, the primitive equalizer, to reclaim Rima's forest. Abel is, bit by bit, deprived of the accoutrements of civilization that he thinks are merely the trappings of his own superior nature, so that at the end, he must survive without even the advantage of a group working towards a single purpose.

It is unclear why Nuflo, the old man, stays in the forest. In part, he stays to fulfill his promise to Rima's mother, but Rima seems perfectly capable of taking care of herself. He seems to be there primarily as a chaperone between Rima and Abel during their "indoor" scenes. Later in the book, it is made clear that Nuflo considers Rima capable of interceding on his behalf with her mother, who Rima believes is in heaven looking down on her, listening to the birdlike speech that only the two of them, Rima and her mother, can understand.

Hudson constructed a carefully hierarchical order in which Rima, in complete harmony with nature, is also the closest to heaven. Abel, with his civilized upbringing, is the only reasonable suitor to such a creature. Nuflo, with his ability to speak Spanish, is nevertheless prone to superstition and lying in his own self-interest, and so takes third place. The Indians, portrayed as treacherous and incapable of grasping any ideas higher than their own physical well-being, fall a distant last.

Yet, if Nature is the highest ideal, why don't the Indians, who must wrest a living from the forest on its own terms, come before Abel and Nuflo? And why doesn't Abel, with his conceit and trappings of the city life, fall last? Maybe this is why the novel bothered me so, and why I failed to perceive the warning signs of Rima's impending death. It would have made a lot more sense to me if Rima had formed an alliance with one of the native boys, and Abel had stumbled on down the trail to further adventures. Belatedly, we are even told of the fiancée he left behind when he falls for Rima, and he spends about fifteen minutes regretting that he plans to abandon her for the bird-girl.

Interestingly, Ronner's biography tells us that Hudson himself had married a birdlike woman, Emily Wingrave, "so tiny that when she stands on the floor she cannot look over the edge of the dinner table."[15] She was fifteen or twenty years older than Hudson, a professional singer who lost her voice shortly after their marriage. None of his literary friends could figure out what he saw in her, but she was clearly the model for several of Hudson's heroines, tiny guardians of Nature Ronner describes as "pre-Eve women."[16]

Hudson and Wingrave stuck together, until her death, through many years of poverty until Hudson finally achieved success. Wingrave accompanied him on many of the countryside rambles that were the source for his books on birds and an idealized view of country living. Like Thomas Hardy, Hudson saw in simple country people an integrity that transcended the institutions of English society. His novel *Fan: The Story of a Young Girl's Life*[17] is the only one in which he deliberately explores the urban English underclass. Other books such as *Hampshire Days*, *A Hind in Richmond Park*, and *A Shepherd's Life* glorify the country way of living.

Hudson's most notable contribution was probably his support of campaigns against the killing of birds for ornamenting women's hats and clothing. Long before PETA, he wrote impassioned diatribes on behalf of various conservation groups that portrayed the brutality of hunters who pulled the valuable wings off of living birds, leaving them to die in agony. He met regularly with other nature lovers and members of the Bird Society.[18]

Hudson, the compulsive classifier of human and avian behavior, deliberately tried to avoid classification himself. He called himself a "religious atheist,"[19] but used a lot of biblical imagery in his stories. While intrigued by Darwinism, he refused to accept it completely. He continued to hold nature as the highest ideal, and seemed to draw whatever religious feelings he had from his interactions with nature. By blurring the lines between the poet and the scientist, he anticipated the current movement within scientific circles to acknowledge the effect of the observer on the observed, which, at least in the social sciences, has changed the way in which data is interpreted.

At that time, most people who read or heard of Darwin's theories thought of themselves, naturally, as the most evolved product of nature. There was even a companion theory of atavism, promulgated by the Italian psychiatrist Cesare Lombroso in his book *Criminal Man*,[20] contending that primitive living conditions favored the criminal mind. This attitude suffuses much of the anthropological research of the era, which includes most of the first descriptions of indigenous people in the western United States, the Pacific, and Australia. The spottiness and self-contradictory aspects of Hudson's own philosophy may account for the flaws in *Green Mansions*, yet most people to this day read the book as both a great environmental novel and a great love story. It was even made into a poorly reviewed movie in 1959 starring Audrey Hepburn and Anthony Perkins.[21]

Hudson's work was promoted by his contemporaries Ford Madox Ford; John Galsworthy, who wrote the preface to the American edition of *Green Mansions;* and the English critic Edward Garnett. Others, such as the novelist and critic Morley Roberts, elevated Hudson to a sort of cult figure: "There was something in his character which forbade him to abandon his soul to others. He kept it in a strong secret place, as those fabled giants in ancient myths keep theirs." Even Ezra Pound referred to a "quiet charm which allures even him through books with seemingly inane titles into worlds which normally wouldn't entice him."[22]

⁘ ⁘ ⁘ ⁘ ⁘

Since first reading *Green Mansions*, I've figured out that a girl of color with romantic aspirations was not the intended audience for this book. Although I now approach novels with a little more caution, I still identify with Rima. Somewhere in Hyde Park, London, is a statue of her sculpted in 1925 by Jacob Epstein. Like her, I feel that there is no place in the world for a woman who talks to birds. Any tree in which I perch is vulnerable to a lighted torch from whatever mob happens to gather around its roots. A pristine mountain lake can suddenly become a killing ground. And no sweet-talking man is going to save me with his birthright.

There is, in this modern or postmodern time, no room for the mystic, no market niche. There is only the clamor of commerce, the knocking together of the pots and pans of overt sexuality from which any spiritual yearnings have been carefully excised, the photographic negative of Hudson's idylls. Rima is nobody's hero today because she meant too much. She embodied a woman who was both physical and spiritual, a strong individualist who was, nevertheless, an innocent. She is described as birdlike, but is, more specifically, angel-like. Unlike the otherworldly half-breeds in Zena Henderson's novels, Hudson could not allow such a transcendent being to also experience carnal love.

What Hudson taught me is that girls who live in trees can never afford to trust others. The daughters of the Didi must guard themselves if they intend to stay alive. Each child, upon coming of age, must set out into the woods without the protection of a parent. What will she find? A wolf in grandmother's clothing, a fox in a tree, a burning bush — *her* burning bush, with all its splendor, and all its terror.

The Desert Remembers My Name

In our ending is our beginning. We gather to close the circle and remember our children and our ancestors. In *Spirits of the Ordinary*, Tomás explains to Zacarías that the desert before them was once an ocean floor—that the lizards and frogs that populate the landscape were once fish and sea creatures. This thought makes Zacarías dizzy with the image of leviathans circling between the cliffs where they sit eating their midday meal.[1]

This thought makes me dizzy, too. In this desert was my beginning. My ancestors were born here, lived and loved here, suffered loss here, and died. Eventually, war scattered us, and we have lived a sort of exile ever since. But in our exile, the stories of the desert have taken on mythic qualities. Nothing else can ever fill up the empty place in our hearts left when we departed this place. Only the deserts and the oceans, the places where the rhythms of the universe are most apparent, can assuage that ache for a few moments.

In *The Flower in the Skull*,[2] a young woman, drowning in her life in Los Angeles, finds herself seeking the answer to the mystery of her origins. She, too, is drawn back to the desert in order to unravel the past. What Shelly finds is a place, at last, to tell her own story, something she has never been given before. She receives the opportunity to plant the seeds of a new life.

I would like to close with a quote from a book published in 1679. It was written by another exile, a Jew named Isaac Cardoso, who left Spain in order to practice his religion. He gave up a position of power and prestige as a doctor in the Spanish Court because his faith was even greater. "*El que me esparció me recogerá,*" he wrote. "He who scatters me will harvest me."[3]

With our dreams, with our stories, with our tears, and with our hopes, we, too, scatter new seeds and harvest new beginnings. We gather outside—the sky above us, the earth below, and all of the ancestors watching. We gather in a place blessed by the sun, watered by the rain, and cooled by the wind. We gather in a place that has known fire, and survived. We are here to remember the future, and look forward to the time when the ancestors remember us. May they rejoice.

The Border Book Festival
Las Cruces, New Mexico
Friday, March 24, 2000

Notes

Día de los Muertos en Tepotzlán

1. Elizabeth Carmichael and Chloe Sayer, *The Skeleton at the Feast* (Austin: University of Texas Press, 1992).

When Do You Sing?

1. "¡Cuán Grande es El!" ("O Mighty God, How Great Thou Art") (Lillenas Publishing Company, 1958).

Vipiniguat-Ru

1. Kathleen Alcalá, *The Flower in the Skull* (San Francisco: Chronicle Books, 1998).

2. Carl Lumholtz, *Among Cannibals: Four Years Travels in Australia* (New York: Charles Scribners, 1889).

3. Ibid., *Unknown Mexico: Explorations in the Sierra Madre and Other Regions, 1890–1898.* 2 vols. (1900; reprint, New York: Dover Publications, 1987).

4. Ibid.

5. Ibid.

6. Jean B. Johnson, *The Opata: An Inland Tribe of Sonora*, Publications in Anthropology Number Six (Albuquerque: University of New Mexico Press, 1950).

7. Ibid.

8. Edward H. Spicer, *Cycles of Conquest* (Tucson and London: University of Arizona Press, 1962).

9. José Cortés, *Views from the Apache Frontier: Report on the Northern Provinces of New Spain, 1799*, translated by John Wheat, edited by Elizabeth A. H. John (Norman: University of Oklahoma Press, 1989).

10. Ramón A. Gutiérrez, *When Jesus Came, the Corn Mothers Went Away* (Stanford, Calif.: Stanford University Press, 1991).

11. Gary Paul Nabhan, numerous books, including *Why Some Like It Hot* (Washington, D.C.: Island Press, 2004).

12. Campbell W. Pennington, "Advertencia," *Vocabulario Opata* (unpublished, Campbell W. Pennington Papers, 1872–, Benson Latin American Collection,

General Libraries, The University of Texas at Austin, and private correspondence with Pennington).

13. Alcalá, *Spirits of the Ordinary* (San Francisco: Chronicle Books, 1997).

14. Johnson, *The Opata.*

More about My Great-Grandmother and the Opata

1. Nicholas J. Bleser, *Tumacacori: From Ranchería to National Monument* (National Park Service Report, undated): 45.

2. Roger C. Owen, *Marobavi: A Study of an Assimilated Group in Northern Sonora* (Tucson: Anthropological Papers of the University of Arizona, no. 3, 1959). Companion volume to Hinton.

3. Thomas Hinton, *A Survey of Indian Assimilation in Eastern Sonora* (Tucson: Anthropological Papers of the University of Arizona, no. 4, 1959).

4. An unpublished interview of Juan Felipe Mayve by Thomas Hinton conducted in 1954, field notes at the Arizona State Museum, Tucson, Arizona.

5. Michael E. Whalen and Paul E. Minnis, *Casas Grandes and Its Hinterland: Regional Organization in Northwest Mexico* (Tucson: University of Arizona Press, 2001).

6. Owen, *Marobavi.*

7. Elizabeth Cook-Lynn, *Why I Can't Read Wallace Stegner and Other Essays* (Madison and London: University of Wisconsin Press, 1996).

8. A. S. Byatt, *On Histories and Stories* (Boston: Harvard University Press, 2001).

Francisco's Library

1. Sheila Bender, editor, *The Writer's Journal* (New York: Dell Publishing, 1997).

The Skeleton in the Closet

1. Leslie Marmon Silko, *Yellow Woman and the Beauty of the Spirit* (New York: Simon and Schuster, 1996).

2. Vito Alessio Robles, *Saltillo en la historia y la leyenda* (Mexico, D.F.: A. Del Bosque, Impresor, 1934).

A Star of David on Christmas

1. Seth D. Kunin, "Juggling Identities among the Crypto-Jews of the American Southwest," *Religion* (2001): 31, 41–61.

2. Miguel Narro, unpublished journals, private collection.

3. Rosa Fe Narro Arrien, *I Married a Priest* (Monterey Park, Calif.: 1951).

4. Ibid., *Sigrid Marries a Catholic* (Monterey Park, Calif., 1954).

5. *The Garden of the Finzi-Continis*, Vittorio De Sica, director, Italy, 1971.

6. www.ccel.org/k/kierkegaard.

7. Victor Perera, *The Cross and the Pear Tree* (New York: Alfred A. Knopf, 1995).

8. Janet Liebman Jacobs, *Hidden Heritage: The Legacy of the Crypto-Jews* (Berkeley and Los Angeles, Calif.: University of California Press, 2002).

A Thread in the Tapestry

1. Alberto y Arturo Garcia Carraffa, *Diccionario Heráldico y Genealógico de Apellidos Españoles y Americanos*, Tomo LIX, Lámina 3a (Barcelona: 1919–1963).

2. Robles, *Saltillo*.

3. *The Raven Chronicles* (Summer/Fall 1992).

4. *Expulsion and Memory: Descendants of the Hidden Jews*, Simcha Jacobovicz and Roger Pyke, directors, Canada, 1996.

5. Ben Nahman, http://home.earthlink.net/bnahman/AtoZlist.htm.

6. *The Atlantic Monthly* (December 2000): 85–96.

Unveiling the Spirits

1. Marta Durón Jimenez y Ignacio Narro Etchegaray, *Los Narro: Origen de una tradicion en el noreste mexicano* (Monterrey, Nuevo León, Mexico: privately published, 1994).

2. Miguel de Cervantes, *Don Quixote de la Mancha*, translated by Edith Grossman (New York: HarperCollins, 2003).

3. Alcalá, "A Thread in the Tapestry: The Narros of Saltillo Mexico in History and Literature," *Halapid* (http://www.cryptojews.com/Alcala.htm).

4. Robles, *Saltillo*.

Spirits of the Ordinary

1. David M. Gitlitz, *Secrecy and Deceit: The Religion of the Crypto-Jews* (Philadelphia: The Jewish Publication Society, 1996): 381–83.

2. Boleslao Lewin, *Los judios bajo la inquisición en hispanoamérica* (Buenos Aires: Editorial Dedalo, 1960).

3. Kathleen Alcalá and Olga Sanchez, *Spirits of the Ordinary* (Portland: The Miracle Theatre, June 2003). Olga Sanchez, director. Published with the permission of Olga Sanchez.

Found in Translation

1. Ignacio Zuñiga, "Opatas," *Rápida ojeada al Estado de Sonora, Territorios de California, y Arizona, año de 1835* (Mexico: Vargas Rea, 1948): 115–33.

Reading the Signs

1. Inéz Hernández Avila, *Reinventing the Enemy's Language*, Joy Harjo and Gloria Bird, editors (New York and London: W. W. Norton and Company, 1997).

2. Gary Paul Nabhan is the author of numerous books on food and our relationship to the environment, including *Gathering the Desert* (Tucson: University of Arizona Press, 1987); *Cultures of Habitat: On Nature, Culture and Story* (Washington, D.C.: Counterpoint, 1997); and *Why Some Like It Hot* (Washington, D.C.: Island Press, 2004).

3. Elizabeth Woody, *Reinventing*.

4. Gutiérrez, *When Jesus Came*.

5. Silko, *Yellow Woman*.

6. Ibid., *Ceremony* (New York: Penguin, 1988).

7. Ibid., *Almanac of the Dead* (New York: Simon and Schuster, 1991).

8. Ibid., *Gardens in the Dunes* (New York: Simon and Schuster, 1999).

The Madonna in Cyberspace

1. C. Vann Woodward, *The Strange Career of Jim Crow* (Commemorative edition; London: Oxford University Press, 2001).

2. Jorge Luis Borges, "The Babylon Lottery," *Ficciones* (English edition; New York: Grove Press, 1969).

3. Anton Chekhov, "The Lady with the Dog," *Anton Chekhov: Five Great Short Stories* (New York: Dover Publications, 1990)

4. James Joyce, *Ulysses* (New York: Random House: The Modern Library, 1934, 1914).

5. Sandra Cisneros, *Woman Hollering Creek* (New York: Vintage Books, 1991).

6. Vi Hilbert interview, *Raven* (Fall 1991): 25.

7. Barry Lopez, lecture, Bainbridge Island, Washington, 2000.

8. Italo Calvino, *The Uses of Literature* (English edition; New York: HBJ, 1982).

9. Audre Lorde, "I Am Your Sister: Black Women Organizing Across Sexualities," in *Making Face, Making Soul/Haciendo Caras*, edited by Gloria Anzaldúa (San Francisco: Aunt Lute Books, 1990).

Against All Odds

1. Alcalá, "La Esmeralda," in *Mrs. Vargas and the Dead Naturalist* (Corvallis, Oreg.: Calyx Books, 1992).

2. Anna Macías, *Against All Odds: The Feminist Movement in Mexico to 1940*, Contributions in Women's Studies Number 30 (Westport, Conn., and London, England: Greenwood Press, 1982).

3. Quoted in Macías, 4–5.

4. Ibid.

5. Ibid.

6. Ibid., 10.

7. Ibid., 13.

8. Ibid.

9. Ibid., 15.

10. Ibid., 16.

11. Ibid.

12. Ibid., 17.

13. Ibid., 13.

14. Ibid., 32.

15. Ibid., 116.

16. Ibid., 145.

17. U.S. Census Bureau, "State Estimates of Organized Child Care Facilities," Lynne M. Casper and Martin O'Connell, Population Division, U.S. Bureau of the Census, Washington, D.C., March 1998, Population Division Working Paper No. 21.

Introduction to *Fantasmas*

1. Rob Johnson, editor, *Fantasmas: Supernatural Stories by Mexican American Writers* (Tempe, Ariz.: Bilingual Press/Editorial Bilingüe, 2001).
2. Alberto Manguel, editor, *Black Water and Black Water 2* (New York: Clarkson N. Potter, 1983, 1990).
3. José García Rodríguez, *Relatos misterio y realismo* (Mexico, 1947).
4. Johnson, *Fantasmas*, 157.
5. *Star Trek*, Gene Roddenberry, producer, television series, 1966–1969.
6. Nicolás Kanellos, "An Overview of Hispanic Literature with Special Emphasis on the Literature of Hispanics in the United States," Multnomah School District 1J (Portland: 1996). "But the real flowering of Spanish-American letters takes place in the contemporary novel as practiced by writers after World War II in what U.S. critics have called a 'boom,' but which Latin Americans refer to as the *nueva narrativa*, or new novel. Its distinguished exponents arise from virtually all of the countries in South and Central America and also in the Caribbean, where the relatively reduced geography of the island of Cuba has contributed such giants to the world of letters as Alejo Carpentier, José Lezama Lima, and Gabriel Cabrera Infante. All contribute to the new sensibility that Carpentier named 'lo real maravilloso' and what the rest of the world soon came to know as 'magic realism.'"
7. National Public Radio interview on Ariel Dorfman's play, *Widows*, November 29, 2001.
8. Johnson, *Fantasmas*, 108.
9. Ibid., 65.
10. Ibid., 35.

The Transforming Eye of Kathleen Alcalá

1. Rob Johnson, American Center for Artists, www.americanartists.org, September 1999. Published with permission from the author.

Words That Heal, Words That Bind

1. Claire Joysmith and Clara Lomas, editors, *One Wound for Another/Una herida por otra: Testimonios de Latin@s in the U.S. through Cyperspace (11 septiembre de 2001–11 marzo de 2002)* (Mexico: Universidad Nacional Autónoma de México, 2005): 90.

Dear John: A Letter to a Friend Following 9/11

1. Claire Joysmith and Clara Lomas, editors, *One Wound for Another/Una herida por otra: Testimonios de Latin@s in the U.S. through Cyperspace (11 septiembre de 2001–11 marzo de 2002)* (Mexico: Universidad Nacional Autónoma de México, 2005): 91.

Present in Our Space

1. *The Seattle Times*, print edition, February 25, 2003, page E-8.
2. Quoted in *Seattle Times*.
3. Larry Vincent Buster, *The Art and History of Black Memorabilia* (New York: Crown Publishing Group, 2000).

4. *Black Ethnic Collectibles*, quarterly (Hyattsville, Md.: BEC).

5. Walter Benjamin, *The Arcades Project* (Boston: Belnap, 1999).

6. *The American Heritage Dictionary*, 2nd edition, s.v. "quodlibet."

7. *LaRousse's French English/English French Dictionary*, s.v. "quolibet."

The Woman Who Loved Water

1. June 20, 2001, quoted in Timothy Roche, "The Yates Odyssey," *Time*, January 28, 2002.

2. Rosemarie Coste, "La Llorona y El Grito/The Ghost and The Scream: Noisy Women in Borderlands and Beyond," Dec. 15, 2000, www.womenwriters .net.

3. Associated Press, Houston, "Mental Decline of Yates Documented," CourtTV.com, *Texas v. Andrea Yates*, February 27, 2002.

4. *New American Standard Bible* (La Habra, California: Foundation Press Publications, 1972).

5. Ellen Makkai, www.ezboard.com, March 23, 2002.

6. "Yates Odyssey," *Time*, 10.

7. "Yates Odyssey," *Time*, 6.

8. Coste, "La Llorona."

9. AP, Houston, "Mental Decline."

10. Coste, "La Llorona."

11. Gloria Anzaldúa, *Borderlands/La Frontera* (San Francisco: Aunt Lute Books, 1999): 76.

12. Anzaldúa, *Prietita and the Ghost Woman/Prietita y la llorona* (San Francisco: Children's Book Press, 1995).

13. Frank Ochberg, *Post-Traumatic Therapy and Victims of Violence* (New York: Brunner/Mazel, 1988).

14. Ochberg, "The Languages of Emotional Injury" (symposium, Seattle University, April 26, 2002).

15. Sandra Cisneros, "Woman Hollering Creek," in *Woman Hollering Creek and Other Stories* (New York: Random House, 1991).

16. Social worker Norma Tauriac, "Yates Odyssey," *Time*, 8.

17. "Yates Odyssey," *Time*, 16.

18. AP, Houston, "Yates Claimed She Killed Kids to Keep Them from Going to Hell," March 1, 2002.

19. *Houston Chronicle*, February 21, 2002.

20. *Standard Bible*, Matthew 18:6.

21. Timothy Roche, "The Devil and Andrea Yates," *Time*, March 11, 2002.

22. Hamida Bosmajian, *Sparing the Child: Children's Literature about Nazism and the Holocaust* (New York: Routledge, 2001).

23. CourtTV.com, March 4, 2002.

24. "Yates Odyssey," *Time*, 16.

25. *Standard Bible*, Revelation 13:6.

26. *Newsweek*, "Michael Woroniecki's Influence over Convicted Murderer Andrea Yates," March 18, 2002.

27. AP, Houston, March 4, 2002.

28. Coste, "La Llorona."

29. Ibid.

30. Ibid.

31. AP, Houston, March 4, 2002.

32. Jim Yardley, "Texas Jury Convicts Mother Who Drowned Her Children," *New York Times*, March 13, 2002.

33. Ibid.

34. Ibid.

35. *Standard Bible*, Genesis 9:15.

36. Rob Johnson, introduction to *Fantasmas*.

37. "The Song of Songs, 1:5,6," *Tanakh*, translated by the Jewish Publication Society, 1985.

38. Ana Castillo, *Massacre of the Dreamers: Essays on Xicanisma* (New York: Plume/Penguin, 1995): 16.

39. Patricia Gonzales, XColumn, Universal Press Syndicate, 2002, www.azteca.net/aztec/literal/xcolumn.html.

40. *Standard Bible*, Romans 6:4.

41. Ed Timms and Diane Jennings, "Guilty Verdict No Surprise Given Texas Laws, Legal Experts Say," *Dallas Morning News*, March 13, 2002.

42. Coste, "La Llorona."

The Girl in the Tree

1. William Henry Hudson, *Green Mansions* (New York: Lancer Books, 1968).

2. Amy D. Ronner, *W. H. Hudson: The Man, the Novelist, the Naturalist* (New York: AMS Press, 1986).

3. Zena Henderson, *Pilgrimage: The Book of the People* (New York: Doubleday, 1952); *The People: No Different Flesh* (New York: Doubleday, 1961).

4. Mary Shelley, *Frankenstein* (1818; reissue edition, New York: Penguin Books, 2003).

5. Hudson, *Green Mansions*, 299.

6. Hudson, *The Purple Land* (New York: Modern Library, 1885, 1904).

7. Hudson, *The Crystal Age* (New York: E. P. Dutton, 1922; reprint, Doric Books, 1950).

8. Robert A. Heinlein, *Have Spacesuit, Will Travel* (New York: Scribner's, 1958).

9. *Star Trek*, Gene Roddenberry, producer, television series, 1966–1969.

10. Jane Austen, *Pride and Prejudice* (London: T. Egerton, 1813).

11. Miguel de Cervantes, *Don Quixote de la Mancha*, Part 1, 1605; Part 2, 1615; translated by Edith Grossman (New York: HarperCollins, 2003).

12. Joan Didion, *Slouching Towards Bethlehem* (New York: Farrar Straus and Giroux, 1968).

13. Hudson, *Crystal Age*, 40.

14. Charles Darwin, *On the Origin of Species* (Norwalk, Conn.: Easton Press, 1859).

15. Ronner, *W. H. Hudson*, 41.

16. Ibid., 61.

17. Hudson, *Fan: The Story of a Young Girl's Life* (London: J. M. Dent & Sons, 1892).

18. Ronner, *W. H. Hudson*, 32, 46.

19. Ibid., 77.

20. Cesare Lombroso, *L'Uomo Delinquente [Criminal Man]* (Milan: Horpli, 1876).

21. *Green Mansions*, Mel Ferrer, director, United States, 1959.

22. Ronner, *W. H. Hudson*, 7, 11.

The Desert Remembers My Name

1. Alcalá, *Spirits*, 54.

2. Alcalá, *Flower*.

3. Reproduced in Yosef Hayim Yerushalmi, *From Spanish Court to Italian Ghetto* (reprint, Seattle and London: University of Washington Press, 1981) title page to Isaac Cardoso's *Las Excellencias de los Hebreos* (Amersterdam: 1679).

About the Author

Kathleen Alcalá is the author of a short-story collection and three novels set in the Southwest and nineteenth-century Mexico. Her work has been favorably reviewed in *The New York Times Book Review* and on National Public Radio, and has received the Pacific Northwest Booksellers Award, the Governor's Writers Award, the Western States Book Award, and the Washington State Book Award.

Kathleen received her B.A. in Human Language from Stanford University and an M.A. in Creative Writing from the University of Washington.

Born in Compton, California, to Mexican parents, she lives near Seattle, Washington. For more information, visit www.kathleen alcala.com.